TILL WE HAVE FACES:
A MYTH RETOLD
by
C.S. Lewis

A Reading Companion

an any day companion for an everyday reader

Christine L. Norvell

Copyright © 2020 Christine L. Norvell

TILL WE HAVE FACES: A MYTH RETOLD – A Reading Companion
Second Edition
By Christine L. Norvell

ISBN-13: 978-0-578-66279-4

Unless otherwise noted, scripture taken from the Holy Bible, English
Standard Version Copyright © 2001 by Crossway, from the Complete
Jewish Bible ® Copyright © 1998 by David H. Stern, Lederer
Messianic Publications.

Cover art by Dan Rempel at *DanRempelIllustration.com.*

Table of Contents

Endorsements

"*Till We Have Faces* is one of Lewis's richest books, but also one of his most challenging. Christine Norvell does readers a great service by offering what is essentially a college course on the novel between two covers. Well researched and smoothly written, Norvell's study guide offers valuable insights in every chapter and encourages readers to actively participate in the act of informed interpretation."

—Dr. David C. Downing, Co-Director of the Marion E. Wade Center, Wheaton College, and author of five books on C. S. Lewis, including the novel *Looking for the King*

"C. S. Lewis called *Till We Have Faces* 'far and away my best book.' In writing and now revising her deeply insightful and very helpful companion, Christine L. Norvell helps readers understand why Lewis thought so, offering excellent guidance to anyone interested in that maddening, magnificent novel."

—Andrew Lazo, C. S. Lewis scholar, editor and transcriber of "Early Prose Joy," Lewis's previously-unknown autobiography, and expert on *Till We Have Faces*

"Christine Novell's illuminating guide on *Till We Have Faces* discusses and untangles many of the enigmatic aspects of this magnificent novel. Norvell herself 'lifts the veil' on one of Lewis's best, but most cryptic, works and illustrates the holy purpose beneath the fictional text."

—Dr. Crystal Hurd, author of *Thirty Days with C.S Lewis: A Women's Devotional* and Reviews Editor for *Sehnsucht: The C.S. Lewis Journal*

"Kudos to Christine Norvell for providing an accessible reading companion that opens up the novel to a wide array of readers. Her analysis and questions zero in on key themes, characters, and symbols in a way that draws out Lewis's meaning rather than imposing her own."

— Dr. Louis Markos, Professor in English and Scholar in Residence, Houston Baptist University; author of *Restoring Beauty: The Good, the True, and the Beautiful in the Writings of C. S. Lewis*

"With a clear vision and a capable hand, Christine Norvell's Reading Companion is a compelling resource inviting readers to draw the mythic beauty of this transformational story into their lives."

— Dr. Brenton D.G. Dickieson, Lecturer and Preceptor, Signum University

"Norvell includes an explanatory chapter for each of the chapters in Lewis' book. Each ends with several thought-provoking and open-ended questions helpful for personal reflection as well as group discussion. Her use of scholarship, primary and secondary, is ample and helpful. I recommend this book for classes, book clubs and church groups. It offers scholarship that is both wise and clarifying."

—Dr. Nancy Enright, Professor of English, Director of University Core, Seton Hall University, and author of *Community: A Reader for Writers* and articles in *Logos*, *Commonweal*, and *The Chesterton Review*

To my most precious family of five.

To my heavenly Father for loving me wholly,
for listening to me, for speaking to me in daily bread portions.

Acknowledgments

Where I am ever a student, I thank Dr. Brenton Dickieson and Andrew Lazo for graciously adding to my knowledge of all things Lewis and for providing needed clarity to the argument of my Introduction. Both men gave generously of their time and experience to help me, an understudy.

With gratitude to the many scholars and thinkers who have gone before me, most especially Peter J. Schakel for his spiritual and academic insights that shaped my thoughts and my classroom discussions.

Without the laboratory of the classroom, my studies, thoughts, and questions would be incomplete. Thank you to Regent Preparatory School for preparing me to write.

"To construct plausible and moving 'other worlds' you must draw on the only real 'other world' we know, that of the spirit." —C.S. Lewis, "On Stories"

Introduction

HOW WE READ

Our perspectives do affect the meaning of what we read. If one of my students were to say the fairy tale "Beauty and the Beast" was about the influence of family, another student might insist that the tale was about how people are monsters. Neither is wrong, but neither is exclusive. Meaning comes to us in many ways.

No reader doubts that our own life experiences create a lens through which we see the world and the words we read. This is the primary way meaning arrives. C.S. Lewis says, "Each of us by nature sees the whole world from one point of view with a perspective and a selectiveness peculiar to himself."[1] Our limitation is natural, and it is helpful to be aware of it.

How then do we approach C.S. Lewis's final novel, *Till We Have Faces*? Many critics at the time complained that it was too different from his previous fiction, that the story was too dark or ambiguous. T.H. White, for example, said the final section was full of "metaphysical mumbo-jumbo."[2] Charles Rolo wrote that "A single reading left some of the novel's meanings obscure."[3] The story invites extremes, and that is our challenge in finding meaning. One approach is to draw from the pool of literary criticism as we consider the types of perspectives readers might share.

---

[1] C.S. Lewis, "Epilogue," in *An Experiment in Criticism* (Cambridge: Cambridge University Press, 1961), 203.

[2] Quoted in Walter Hooper, *C.S. Lewis: A Complete Guide to His Life & Works* (San Francisco: HarperCollins, 1996), 262.

[3] *Ibid.*

Experts who think about the way we read literature also think about different kinds of perspectives. With the Reader-Response theory of literary criticism, for example, the meaning of the story rests with us, the readers. Meaning comes to us as we interact with the text.

When we ask if the sound and shape of word and phrase are important or if the order of the words within a sentence carries meaning, we champion careful reading, but it is also about thoughtful reflection within the reader's involvement with the words. These are elements of Reader-Response theory and they are strengths to the reader. The implied question of course is whether the interaction between the reader and the text is the *only* source of meaning.

What if we were to consider New Criticism, most popular after World War I? Its distinct claim is to look at a literary work as a piece of art. Having coined the term "New Criticism" in 1910, J.E. Spingarn clarifies that "the poet's aim must be judged at the moment of the creative act, that is to say, by the art of the poem itself."[4] Its beauty is in the creation.

Lewis would call this *poiema* or something made. He explains, "As Poiema, by its aural beauties and also by the balance and contrast and the unified multiplicity of its successive parts, it is an *objet d'art*, a thing shaped so as to give great satisfaction."[5] Thus, the poet or creator leads us to look at the art he has created.

Under this theory we would then ask what the story's value is as an independent piece, regardless of the author, genre, or time period. It's a fascinating and simplifying perspective. I could then look at *The Little Prince*, for example, as an important picture of childlikeness. I don't need to identify the genre of the story or analyze the life of Antoine de Saint-Exupéry to see that we should

---

[4] Spingarn, "The New Criticism" in *Criticism in America, Its Function and Status: Essays*. W.C. Brownell, et al. (New York: Harcourt, 1924), 24-25.

[5] *Experiment*, 132.

all be sensitive to the beauty around us and be willing to question why things in the world are done the way they are.

But literary theory is only one approach with many labels. According to Lewis, meaning is more than names and labels and models. In *The Discarded Image*, he asks us to

> "regard *all* Models in the right way, respecting each
> and idolising none. We are all, very properly,
> familiar with the idea that in every age the human
> mind is deeply influenced by the accepted Model of
> the universe. But there is a two-way traffic; the
> Model is also influenced by the prevailing temper of
> mind."[6]

Lewis continues by clarifying that each model "reflects the prevalent psychology of an age almost as much as it reflects the state of that age's knowledge."[7] I wonder if we should think of it this way: what we read affects us and reflects us even when we are not aware of it.

A more broad approach might include Lewis's concept of *poiema* and *logos*. At the same time we see a piece of literature as art, something made, it is also *logos* or something said. "As Logos it tells a story, or expresses an emotion, or exhorts or pleads or describes or rebukes or excites laughter."[8] The two elements of *poiema* and *logos* work together.

What then would C.S. Lewis say about how to approach his work?

It's most fascinating that one of his earliest books, *The Personal Heresy* (1939), was a series of debates with Dr. E.M.W. Tillyard about how to interpret the poet and their poems. Tillyard

---

[6] *The Discarded Image: An Introduction to Medieval and Renaissance Literature* (Cambridge: Cambridge University Press, 1964), 222.

[7] *Ibid.*

[8] *Experiment, 132.*

had published a book on *Paradise Lost* in 1930 with the premise that "All poetry is about the poet's state of mind." He argued that we learn who John Milton is by reading his work.

Lewis countered this approach, claiming it was a "personal heresy" because it alleged to know the *person* of Milton through his creative words. Lewis felt this biographical approach was too limited and too subjective. Rather, we the readers should share what is common to the poet and to us. We share our human experience, not the author's personality alone. Lewis later describes the author as a window into something. His person is but a starting point, only one element in an objective approach.

Years later, in *An Experiment in Criticism* (1961), Lewis moderated his view. He further asks if we should judge literature by the way people read it.[9] Lewis said if someone has a negative attitude (valid or not) toward a book as they begin reading, they will see it negatively. We, on the other hand, have a choice. He tells us to "empty our minds and lay ourselves open. There is no work in which holes can't be picked; no work that can succeed without a preliminary act of good will on the part of the reader."[10]

We must be cautious when we read between the lines, and every reader does. By nature, we bring our own perspectives, and here we can remember the art of something made, *poiema*, and the expression of something said, the *logos*. Lewis further reasons,

"It matters more to see precisely what sort of poet Homer is than to tell the world how much it ought to like that sort of poet. The best value judgement is that 'which almost insensibly forms itself in a fair and clear mind, along with fresh knowledge.'"[11]

If we the readers must come with a fresh mind, then the value truly lies with us. That's why Lewis tells us to "Find out what the author actually wrote and what the hard words meant and what the allusions were to, and you have done far more for me than a

---

[9] *Ibid.*, 157.

[10] *Experiment*, 174.

[11] Matthew Arnold quoted in *Function of Criticism* in *Experiment*, 179.

hundred new interpretations or assessments could ever do."[12] The work is upon us the reader, and our end game is to see what the author sees, the same view Lewis advocated for in the 1930s.

THE CONTEXT OF C.S. LEWIS'S TIME[13]

Till We Have Faces is a product of decades of thought. In order to understand what Lewis writes, we cannot discount what he brings us or *when* he does. We can unearth layers of meaning this way as long as we acknowledge they are not the only way to understand a piece of literature, for there are many.

And Lewis would want us to understand. In his *Studies in Medieval and Renaissance Literature*, he writes that it would be a waste to see the past and the works therein with just our own faces.

> "So with old literature. You can go beyond the first
> impression that a poem makes on your modern
> sensibility. By study of things outside the poem, by
> comparing it with other poems, by steeping yourself
> in the vanished period, you can then re-enter the
> poem with eyes more like those of the natives; now
> perhaps seeing that the associations you gave to the
> old words were false, that the real implications were
> different than you supposed, that what you thought
> strange was then ordinary and that what seemed to
> you ordinary was then strange..."[14]

---

[12] *Experiment*, 181.

[13] Peter J. Schakel writes extensively about context in *Reason and Imagination in C.S. Lewis: A Study of Till We Have Faces* (Grand Rapids, MI: Eerdmans, 1984).

[14] "On Two Ways of Traveling and Two Ways of Reading" in *Studies in Medieval and Renaissance Literature* (Cambridge: Cambridge University Press, 1980), 3.

Lewis's lifetime (1898-1963) is far from a vanished period, and this is to our advantage as readers. I say it again, *when* Lewis wrote might be just as important as what he wrote.

Lewis was enamored of the myth of Cupid and Psyche as early as 1917. By 1922, Lewis attempted to find a form for the myth. He wrote 156 lines of rhyming couplets, rewriting the Psyche story, a fragment preserved in "The Lewis Papers" collection at the Marion E. Wade Center at Wheaton College.

Diana Pavlac Glyer points out another critical component. When Lewis had first attempted the story, he was an atheist. He even says "In my pre-Christian days she [Orual] was to be in the right, and the gods in the wrong."[15] But, writing now as a Christian, Lewis "changed the very center of the story, from an angry and justified accusation of the gods to a new awareness that the problem lies with us."[16]

It wasn't until his later years that Lewis was free to write further about the lingering idea. By 1955, the Inklings were no longer meeting in his rooms at Magdalen College, Oxford, or as regularly at the Eagle and Child pub. In January, he began his lecturing duties at Cambridge as Professor of Medieval and Renaissance Literature, a position created specifically for him. Without tutorials, Lewis had more leisure to write. In March of that year Joy Davidman described his leisure as

> "...no pupils, no exams, no college meetings; just a
> nice quiet room and all the time in the world. So the
> inevitable happened; he's dried up. He is quite
> worried about it, and was relieved to know it's the
> usual thing in our trade. I imagine, though, he'll be

---

[15] Quoted in Hooper, *C.S. Lewis: A Complete Guide,* 248-249.

[16] Diana Pavlac Glyer. "Joy Davidman Lewis: Author, Editor and Collaborator," *Mythlore: A Journal of J.R.R. Tolkien, C.S. Lewis, Charles Williams, and Mythopoeic Literature* 22, no.2 (1998): 13.

turning out fiction soon again."[17]

A week later Joy Davidman writes of Lewis's quandary again when she visited the Kilns.

> "One night he was lamenting that he couldn't get a good idea for a book. We kicked a few ideas around until one came to life. Then we had another whiskey each and bounced it back and forth between us. The next day, without further planning, he wrote the first chapter! I read it and made some criticisms (feels quite like old times); he did it over and went on with the next."[18]

An accomplished poet and writer, Davidman did bring insight to his ideas. She greatly enjoyed the editing process as she helped Jack's brother Warnie and others with their manuscripts. Lewis's publisher Jocelyn Gibbs reached out to Davidman as well to help with editing questions for *Surprised by Joy*. Her son Douglas Gresham later stated that she was Jack's editor and that Jack wanted her name on *Till We Have Faces*. Davidman refused, saying, "I can tell him how to write more like himself!"[19] And she did. Many scholars note her influence in the realism of the central female character of Orual.[20]

Lewis wrote just as prolifically in this later period. Amid numerous essays, Lewis completed his exhaustive text *Poetry and Prose in the Sixteenth Century* in 1954 as well as concluding the Narniad in 1955 and 1956 with *The Magician's Nephew* and *The Last Battle*. His autobiography *Surprised by Joy* was released in

---

[17] Joy Davidman to William Lindsay Gresham, March 16, 1955 in *Out of My Bone: The Letters of Joy Davidman.* Ed. Don W. King (Grand Rapids, MI: Eerdmans, 2009), 241.

[18] Joy Davidman to William Lindsay Gresham, March 23, 1955, 242.

[19] Joy Davidman to William Lindsay Gresham, April 29, 1955, 246.

[20] Glyer, "Joy Davidman Lewis," 15.

1955, *Till We Have Faces* in 1956, and *Reflections on the Psalms* in 1958. By 1960, Lewis published *The Four Loves*, examining the nature of love through a journey of definitions along with love's four Greek meanings.

In more than one personal letter Lewis mentions how his protagonist Orual in *Till We Have Faces* struggled with learning the nature of love. In his introduction to *The Four Loves*, he astutely describes how

> "We may give our human loves the unconditional
> allegiance which we owe only to God. Then they
> become gods: then they become demons. Then they
> will destroy us, and also destroy themselves. For
> natural loves that are allowed to become gods do not
> remain loves. They are still called so, but can
> become in fact complicated forms of hatred."[21]

More than idolatry, misplaced love destroys. And it is Lewis's treatment of "devouring love" that is very much a part of *Till We Have Faces*. In a letter to a friend, Lewis wrote "The main themes are (1) Natural affection, if left to mere nature, easily becomes a special kind of hatred, (2) God is, to our natural affections, the ultimate object of jealousy."[22] That is why reading *The Four Loves* alongside *Till We Have Faces* is so helpful.

All four loves do play a role in the story, whether in their ideal form or as a distortion. Any one of these can become an idol, a rival for God. Simply put, they cannot "do what they promise to do without God's help" (152).

---

[21] *The Four Loves* (New York: Harcourt, 1960), 10. *The Four Loves* is hereafter noted in the text.

[22] C.S. Lewis to Father Peter Milward SJ, September 24, 1959, in Hooper 250.

The first three are what Lewis terms natural loves.

(1) Affection is a humble love. It is the warm comfort, the satisfaction of being together as family members. It is unique in that it weaves through the other three loves as well (42-45).

(2) The next love is Friendship, one the ancients valued highly. Friendship is the least jealous and "utterly free from Affection's need to be needed" (78,89) because it appreciates and cares about the same truths.

(3) The third love is *Eros*. It is not sexual instinct alone but rather the desire for the Beloved because it "obliterates the distinction between giving and receiving" (121,123). It is not lust but can be "the body's share in marriage which, by God's choice, is the mystical image of the union between God and man" (126).

(4) The final love is Charity, a "Divine Gift-love—Love Himself working in a man—is wholly disinterested and desires what is best for the beloved" (164). It allows us, mankind, to love the unlovable at the same time that He enables us to have a Need-love for Him. Affection, Friendship, and Eros become "the modes of Charity" (171).

When troubles come, when we are weak, we realize that one of these natural loves is not enough to help us. When we are in situations that require "forbearance, tolerance, forgiveness. The necessity of practising these virtues first sets us, forces us, upon the attempt to turn—more strictly, to let God turn—our love into Charity" (173). Lewis calls it a conversion whereby our natural loves turn towards the heavenly, just as "those into which Love Himself has entered will ascend to Love Himself" (174).

THE CONTEXT OF MYTH

In the preface to the 1956 British edition of *Till We Have Faces*, Lewis writes, "This re-interpretation of an old story has lived in the author's mind, thickening and hardening with the years, ever since he was an undergraduate. That way, he could be said to have worked at it most of his life. Recently, what seemed to be the right form presented itself and themes suddenly interlocked." The form was myth. Glyer writes Lewis "hit upon the right form and a new purpose."[23]

According to Lewis, myth is a structure, a form to convey understanding to potentially any age reader. "It can give us experiences we have never had and thus, instead of 'commenting on life,' can add to it."[24]

As myth then, *Till We Have Faces* is not about theology. In his review of J.R.R. Tolkien's *The Fellowship of the Ring*, Lewis clarifies, "What shows that we are reading myth, not allegory, is that there are no pointers to a specifically theological, or political, or psychological application. A myth points, for each reader, to the realm he lives in most. It is a master key; use it on what door you like."[25] This is because it does something to us at a deep level.[26]

Another way to think of it is that myth is a tool. In the same essay, Lewis explains that the world of myth removes the familiar much like G.K. Chesterton's idea of elementary wonder. "We all like astonishing tales because they touch the nerve of the ancient instinct of astonishment."[27] They startle us from routine and hopefully awaken our understanding of the people and world about us.

But more than that, myth restores a richness. "If you are tired of the real landscape, look at it in a mirror. By putting bread, gold, horse, apple, or the very roads into a myth, we do not retreat from reality: we rediscover it. As long as the story lingers in our mind,

---

[23] Glyer, "Joy Davidman Lewis," 13.

[24] Lewis, "Sometimes Fairy Stories May Say Best What's To Be Said," 48.

[25] Lewis, "Tolkien's *The Lord of the Rings*," 85.

[26] Lewis, "On Science Fiction," 67.

[27] G.K. Chesterton. "The Ethics of Elfland," in *Orthodoxy* (London: John Lane Company, 1908), 95-6.

the real things are more themselves...By dipping them in myth we see them more clearly."[28]

Lewis adds to that layer by giving his myth a historical setting. He places it in a small ancient kingdom that knows of classical Greece. But Glome is far enough away to make Greece a distant place. There is no need for a set historical time within the story. In his oft-quoted letter to friend Clyde Kilby, Lewis clarifies that the novel is "a work of (supposed) *historical* imagination. A guess at what it might have been like in a little barbarous state on the borders of the Hellenistic world with Greek culture just beginning to affect it."[29] The time period is both vague and ancient much like the mythical Narnia.

And this mythic style is also reflected in Lewis's writing. He writes as Orual, a queen near death, writing in an ancient time in a language not her own because she was taught to use Greek. Thus unlike the space trilogy or the Narnia Chronicles, Lewis's storytelling here feels different from his other fiction.

Lewis believed that myth is able to invite us into a story, reveal things we didn't know about ourselves, and ultimately illuminate truth. Finally, just as we have talked about how perspective shapes our reading and understanding, so does perspective and perception become critical to our central character Orual and to understanding the story as a whole.

---

[28] Lewis, "Tolkien," 90.

[29] Clyde S. Kilby. *The Christian World of C.S. Lewis* (Grand Rapids, MI: Eerdman's, 1964), 57-58.

Preface

I will incline my ear and consent to a proverb;
On the harp, I will unfold my riddle.
—Psalm 49:4 (Amp)

HAVING TAUGHT THE novel for more than a decade, I'm still surprised when C.S. Lewis fans mention to me that they don't get the story. More than once, I've heard "How could this be Lewis's favorite? Why?" Or "I like the first part of the story, but the second part is so ambiguous." Or the saddest confession, "I know I didn't understand the story."

I could present an academic analysis to satisfy those questions and join others culling opinions and research, but a definitive guide is not my intent. When I first began teaching the novel years ago, I learned alongside my students. There were few, if any, teaching guides published then, and I eventually wondered if I could repair that.

I hope to reach those who are reading Lewis for the first time. And I hope to be a help by adding the work of others to this second edition. As Lewis explains in his preface to *The Discarded Image,* his desire was not to take you "*out* of the literature itself," forcing you to stop reading in order to research. His hope and mine is "that if a tolerable (though very incomplete) outfit were acquired beforehand and taken along with one, it might lead *in*."[30]

That's why my desire is to be your "outfit," your companion as we read together in our own one-on-one book club if you will. Part summary, part commentary, and a touch of analysis.

Though my classes are generally familiar with the myth of Cupid and Psyche, you may not be. Some scholars say it's best to

---

[30] Lewis, *The Discarded Image,* xi.

read it last, after the novel. Others feel it's helpful to recognize what Lewis changes in the story, especially where he adds to it. Walter Hooper says that Lewis's version will be clearer "if the reader has some notion of the story he [Lewis] was re-interpreting."[31]

Lewis was partial to one of the earliest Greek versions from the second century by Apuleius, who Lewis credits as a source but not a model for his story. In the medieval tradition, Lewis is a renovator of the myth. Most editions include Lewis's end note containing his shortened version and his comments on the "central alteration" he makes. There Lewis says, "I feel quite free to go behind Apuleius, whom I suppose to have been its [the story's] transmitter, not its inventor."

If you'd like, in preparation for the novel, take a few minutes to read Lewis's version in the end note or to read a longer, more storied version here.

CUPID AND PSYCHE[32]

A CERTAIN KING and queen had three daughters. The charms of the two elder were more than common, but the beauty of the youngest was so wonderful that the poverty of language is unable to express its due praise. The fame of her beauty was so great that strangers from neighboring countries came in crowds to enjoy the sight, and looked on her with amazement, paying her that homage which is due only to Venus herself. In fact Venus found her altars deserted, while men turned their devotion to this young virgin. As she passed along, the people sang her praises, and strewed her way with chaplets and flowers.

This perversion of homage due only to the immortal powers to the exaltation of a mortal gave great offence to the real Venus. Shaking her ambrosial locks with indignation, she exclaimed, "Am

---

[31] Hooper, *C.S. Lewis: A Complete Guide*, 244.

[32] Bulfinch, Thomas. *The Age of Fable*. New York: Review of Reviews, 1913; Bartleby.com, 2000. www.bartleby.com/bulfinch/

I then to be eclipsed in my honors by a mortal girl? In vain then did that royal shepherd, whose judgment was approved by Jove himself, give me the palm of beauty over my illustrious rivals, Pallas and Juno. But she shall not so quietly usurp my honors. I will give her cause to repent of so unlawful a beauty."

Thereupon she calls her winged son Cupid, mischievous enough in his own nature, and rouses and provokes him yet more by her complaints. She points out Psyche to him and says, "My dear son, punish that contumacious beauty; give thy mother a revenge as sweet as her injuries are great; infuse into the bosom of that haughty girl a passion for some low, mean, unworthy being, so that she may reap a mortification as great as her present exultation and triumph."

Cupid prepared to obey the commands of his mother. There are two fountains in Venus's garden, one of sweet waters, the other of bitter. Cupid filled two amber vases, one from each fountain, and suspending them from the top of his quiver, hastened to the chamber of Psyche, whom he found asleep. He shed a few drops from the bitter fountain over her lips, though the sight of her almost moved him to pity; then touched her side with the point of his arrow. At the touch she awoke, and opened eyes upon Cupid (himself invisible), which so startled him that in his confusion he wounded himself with his own arrow. Heedless of his wound, his whole thought now was to repair the mischief he had done, and he poured the balmy drops of joy over all her silken ringlets.

Psyche, henceforth frowned upon by Venus, derived no benefit from all her charms. True, all eyes were cast eagerly upon her, and every mouth spoke her praises; but neither king, royal youth, nor plebeian presented himself to demand her in marriage. Her two elder sisters of moderate charms had now long been married to two royal princes; but Psyche, in her lonely apartment, deplored her solitude, sick of that beauty which, while it procured abundance of flattery, had failed to awaken love.

Her parents, afraid that they had unwittingly incurred the anger of the gods, consulted the oracle of Apollo, and received this answer: "The virgin is destined for the bride of no mortal lover. Her future husband awaits her on the top of the mountain. He is a monster whom neither gods nor men can resist."

This dreadful decree of the oracle filled all the people with dismay, and her parents abandoned themselves to grief. But Psyche said, "Why, my dear parents, do you now lament me? You should rather have grieved when the people showered upon me undeserved honors, and with one voice called me a Venus. I now perceive that I am a victim to that name. I submit. Lead me to that rock to which my unhappy fate has destined me." Accordingly, all things being prepared, the royal maid took her place in the procession, which more resembled a funeral than a nuptial pomp, and with her parents, amid the lamentations of the people, ascended the mountain, on the summit of which they left her alone, and with sorrowful hearts returned home.

While Psyche stood on the ridge of the mountain, panting with fear and with eyes full of tears, the gentle Zephyr raised her from the earth and bore her with an easy motion into a flowery dale. By degrees her mind became composed, and she laid herself down on the grassy bank to sleep. When she awoke refreshed with sleep, she looked round and beheld near by a pleasant grove of tall and stately trees. She entered it, and in the midst discovered a fountain, sending forth clear and crystal waters, and fast by, a magnificent palace whose august front impressed the spectator that it was not the work of mortal hands, but the happy retreat of some god. Drawn by admiration and wonder, she approached the building and ventured to enter. Every object she met filled her with pleasure and amazement. Golden pillars supported the vaulted roof, and the walls were enriched with carvings and paintings representing beasts of the chase and rural scenes, adapted to delight the eye of the beholder. Proceeding onward, she perceived that besides the apartments of state there were others filled with all manner of treasures, and beautiful and precious productions of nature and art.

While her eyes were thus occupied, a voice addressed her, though she saw no one, uttering these words: "Sovereign lady, all that you see is yours. We whose voices you hear are your servants and shall obey all your commands with our utmost care and diligence. Retire, therefore, to your chamber and repose on your bed of down, and when you see fit repair to the bath. Supper awaits you in the adjoining alcove when it pleases you to take your seat there."

Psyche gave ear to the admonitions of her vocal attendants, and after repose and the refreshment of the bath, seated herself in the alcove, where a table immediately presented itself, without any visible aid from waiters or servants, and covered with the greatest delicacies of food and the most nectareous wines. Her ears too were feasted with music from invisible performers; of whom one sang, another played on the lute, and all closed in the wonderful harmony of a full chorus.

She had not yet seen her destined husband. He came only in the hours of darkness and fled before the dawn of morning, but his accents were full of love, and inspired a like passion in her. She often begged him to stay and let her behold him, but he would not consent. On the contrary he charged her to make no attempt to see him, for it was his pleasure, for the best of reasons, to keep concealed. "Why should you wish to behold me?" he said; "have you any doubt of my love? have you any wish ungratified? If you saw me, perhaps you would fear me, perhaps adore me, but all I ask of you is to love me. I would rather you would love me as an equal than adore me as a god."

This reasoning somewhat quieted Psyche for a time, and while the novelty lasted she felt quite happy. But at length the thought of her parents, left in ignorance of her fate, and of her sisters, precluded from sharing with her the delights of her situation, preyed on her mind and made her begin to feel her palace as but a splendid prison. When her husband came one night, she told him her distress, and at last drew from him an unwilling consent that her sisters should be brought to see her.

So, calling Zephyr, she acquainted him with her husband's commands, and he, promptly obedient, soon brought them across the mountain down to their sister's valley. They embraced her and she returned their caresses. "Come," said Psyche, "enter with me my house and refresh yourselves with whatever your sister has to offer." Then taking their hands she led them into her golden palace, and committed them to the care of her numerous train of attendant voices, to refresh them in her baths and at her table, and to show them all her treasures. The view of these celestial delights caused envy to enter their bosoms, at seeing their young sister possessed of such state and splendor, so much exceeding their own.

They asked her numberless questions, among others what sort of a person her husband was. Psyche replied that he was a beautiful youth, who generally spent the daytime in hunting upon the mountains. The sisters, not satisfied with this reply, soon made her confess that she had never seen him. Then they proceeded to fill her bosom with dark suspicions. "Call to mind," they said, "the Pythian oracle that declared you destined to marry a direful and tremendous monster. The inhabitants of this valley say that your husband is a terrible and monstrous serpent, who nourishes you for a while with dainties that he may by and by devour you. Take our advice. Provide yourself with a lamp and a sharp knife; put them in concealment that your husband may not discover them, and when he is sound asleep, slip out of bed, bring forth your lamp, and see for yourself whether what they say is true or not. If it is, hesitate not to cut off the monster's head, and thereby recover your liberty."

Psyche resisted these persuasions as well as she could, but they did not fail to have their effect on her mind, and when her sisters were gone, their words and her own curiosity were too strong for her to resist. So she prepared her lamp and a sharp knife, and hid them out of sight of her husband. When he had fallen into his first sleep, she silently rose and uncovering her lamp beheld not a hideous monster, but the most beautiful and charming of the gods, with his golden ringlets wandering over his snowy neck and crimson cheek, with two dewy wings on his shoulders, whiter than snow, and with shining feathers like the tender blossoms of spring. As she leaned the lamp over to have a nearer view of his face a drop of burning oil fell on the shoulder of the god, startled with which he opened his eyes and fixed them full upon her; then, without saying one word, he spread his white wings and flew out of the window. Psyche, in vain endeavoring to follow him, fell from the window to the ground. Cupid, beholding her as she lay in the dust, stopped his flight for an instant and said, "O foolish Psyche, is it thus you repay my love? After having disobeyed my mother's commands and made you my wife, will you think me a monster and cut off my head? But go; return to your sisters, whose advice you seem to think preferable to mine. I inflict no other punishment on you than to leave you forever. Love cannot dwell with suspicion." So saying, he fled away, leaving poor Psyche prostrate on the ground, filling the place with mournful lamentations.

When she had recovered some degree of composure she looked around her, but the palace and gardens had vanished, and she found herself in the open field not far from the city where her sisters dwelt. She repaired thither and told them the whole story of her misfortunes, at which, pretending to grieve, those spiteful creatures inwardly rejoiced. "For now," said they, "he will perhaps choose one of us." With this idea, without saying a word of her intentions, each of them rose early the next morning and ascended the mountains, and having reached the top, called upon Zephyr to receive her and bear her to his lord; then leaping up, and not being sustained by Zephyr, fell down the precipice and was dashed to pieces.

Psyche meanwhile wandered day and night, without food or repose, in search of her husband. Casting her eyes on a lofty mountain having on its brow a magnificent temple, she sighed and said to herself, "Perhaps my love, my lord, inhabits there," and directed her steps thither.

She had no sooner entered than she saw heaps of corn, some in loose ears and some in sheaves, with mingled ears of barley.

Scattered about, lay sickles and rakes, and all the instruments of harvest, without order, as if thrown carelessly out of the weary reapers' hands in the sultry hours of the day.

This unseemly confusion the pious Psyche put an end to, by separating and sorting everything to its proper place and kind, believing that she ought to neglect none of the gods, but endeavor by her piety to engage them all in her behalf. The holy Ceres, whose temple it was, finding her so religiously employed, thus spoke to her: "O Psyche, truly worthy of our pity, though I cannot shield you from the frowns of Venus, yet I can teach you how best to allay her displeasure. Go, then, and voluntarily surrender yourself to your lady and sovereign, and try by modesty and submission to win her forgiveness, and perhaps her favor will restore you the husband you have lost."

Psyche obeyed the commands of Ceres and took her way to the temple of Venus, endeavoring to fortify her mind and ruminating on what she should say and how best propitiate the angry goddess, feeling that the issue was doubtful and perhaps fatal.

Venus received her with angry countenance. "Most undutiful and faithless of servants," said she, "do you at last remember that you really have a mistress? Or have you rather come to see your sick husband, yet laid up of the wound given him by his loving wife? You are so ill-favored and disagreeable that the only way you can merit your lover must be by dint of industry and diligence. I will make trial of your housewifery." Then she ordered Psyche to be led to the storehouse of her temple, where was laid up a great quantity of wheat, barley, millet, vetches, beans, and lentils prepared for food for her pigeons, and said, "Take and separate all these grains, putting all of the same kind in a parcel by themselves, and see that you get it done before evening." Then Venus departed and left her to her task.

But Psyche, in a perfect consternation at the enormous work, sat stupid and silent, without moving a finger to the inextricable heap.

While she sat despairing, Cupid stirred up the little ant, a native of the fields, to take compassion on her. The leader of the ant hill, followed by whole hosts of his six-legged subjects, approached the heap, and with the utmost diligence, taking grain by grain, they separated the pile, sorting each kind to its parcel; and when it was all done, they vanished out of sight in a moment.

Venus at the approach of twilight returned from the banquet of the gods, breathing odors and crowned with roses. Seeing the task done, she exclaimed, "This is no work of yours, wicked one, but his, whom to your own and his misfortune you have enticed." So saying, she threw her a piece of black bread for her supper and went away.

Next morning Venus ordered Psyche to be called and said to her, "Behold yonder grove which stretches along the margin of the water. There you will find sheep feeding without a shepherd, with golden-shining fleeces on their backs. Go, fetch me a sample of that precious wool gathered from every one of their fleeces."

Psyche obediently went to the riverside, prepared to do her best to execute the command. But the river god inspired the reeds with harmonious murmurs, which seemed to say, "O maiden, severely tried, tempt not the dangerous flood, nor venture among the formidable rams on the other side, for as long as they are under the influence of the rising sun, they burn with a cruel rage to destroy mortals with their sharp horns or rude teeth. But when the noontide sun has driven the cattle to the shade, and the serene spirit of the flood has lulled them to rest, you may then cross in safety, and you will find the woolly gold sticking to the bushes and the trunks of the trees."

Thus the compassionate river god gave Psyche instructions how to accomplish her task, and by observing his directions she soon returned to Venus with her arms full of the golden fleece; but she received not the approbation of her implacable mistress, who said, "I know very well it is by none of your own doings that you have succeeded in this task, and I am not satisfied yet that you have any capacity to make yourself useful. But I have another task for you. Here, take this box and go your way to the infernal shades, and give this box to Proserpine and say, 'My mistress Venus desires you to send her a little of your beauty, for in tending her sick son she has lost some of her own.' Be not too long on your errand, for I must paint myself with it to appear at the circle of the gods and goddesses this evening."

Psyche was now satisfied that her destruction was at hand, being obliged to go with her own feet directly down to Erebus. Wherefore, to make no delay of what was not to be avoided, she goes to the top of a high tower to precipitate herself headlong, thus to descend the shortest way to the shades below. But a voice from the tower said to her, "Why, poor unlucky girl, dost thou design to put an end to thy days in so dreadful a manner? And what cowardice makes thee sink under this last danger who hast been so miraculously supported in all thy former?" Then the voice told her how by a certain cave she might reach the realms of Pluto, and how to avoid all the dangers of the road, to pass by Cerberus, the three-headed dog, and prevail on Charon, the ferryman, to take her across the black river and bring her back again. But the voice added, "When Proserpine has given you the box filled with her beauty, of all things this is chiefly to be observed by you, that you never once open or look into the box nor allow your curiosity to pry into the treasure of the beauty of the goddesses."

Psyche, encouraged by this advice, obeyed it in all things, and taking heed to her ways travelled safely to the kingdom of Pluto. She was admitted to the palace of Proserpine, and without accepting the delicate seat or delicious banquet that was offered her, but contented with coarse bread for her food, she delivered her message from Venus. Presently the box was returned to her, shut and filled with the precious commodity. Then she returned the way she came, and glad was she to come out once more into the light of day.

But having got so far successfully through her dangerous task, a longing desire seized her to examine the contents of the box. "What," said she, "shall I, the carrier of this divine beauty, not take the least bit to put on my cheeks to appear to more advantage in the eyes of my beloved husband!" So she carefully opened the box, but found nothing there of any beauty at all, but an infernal and truly Stygian sleep, which being thus set free from its prison, took possession of her, and she fell down in the midst of the road, a sleepy corpse without sense or motion.

Cupid, being now recovered from his wound, and not able longer to bear the absence of his beloved Psyche, slipping through the smallest crack of the window of his chamber which happened to be left open, flew to the spot where Psyche lay, and gathering up the sleep from her body closed it again in the box, and waked Psyche with a light touch of one of his arrows. "Again," said he, "hast thou almost perished by the same curiosity. But now perform exactly the task imposed on you by my mother, and I will take care of the rest."

Then Cupid, as swift as lightning penetrating the heights of heaven, presented himself before Jupiter with his supplication. Jupiter lent a favoring ear, and pleaded the cause of the lovers so earnestly with Venus that he won her consent. On this he sent Mercury to bring Psyche up to the heavenly assembly, and when she arrived, handing her a cup of ambrosia, he said, "Drink this, Psyche, and be immortal; nor shall Cupid ever break away from the knot in which he is tied, but these nuptials shall be perpetual."

Thus Psyche became at last united to Cupid, and in due time they had a daughter born to them whose name was Pleasure.

READING REMINDERS

Each chapter in this edition contains study questions followed by reflection questions for Lewis's developing themes and motifs. Since theme and motif are commonly confused, I offer a few distinctions that have been helpful to my students.

The word *motif* is often used in music to point out a recurring pattern, specifically a melody or musical phrase that is not as prominent as the overall theme. In literature, a motif can be a symbol, image, wording, or even ideas. The motif is always a helper. It contributes to the theme, a broader, more abstract idea.

Along with motifs and themes are Lewis's use of symbols and tools. Symbols simply represent something else, as a red rose might be a symbol for love. Tools, on the other hand, are part of a author's style of writing. Both paradox and irony catch our attention because they cause us to look at something in a new way. John Donne's final line from Holy Sonnet 10 is one brief example of paradox: "Death, thou shalt die." It seems contrary if we ask if death can die. Yet, at death, heaven is imminent, and once we die, death is no more. It is not a morbid thought, but a hopeful one.

Irony is a cousin of sarcasm. It shares a similar contrast because a character might say or do something yet mean another. King Trom, for example, shouts at our central character Orual because she is ugly, then yells at her again because she covered her ugly face. It is ironic because her appearance can never please him, and in fact, he doesn't "see" who she is as a person anyway.

THEMES

Love and its types
Longing
Joy
Sacrifice
Justice
Seeing
Perception
Belief
Faith
Beauty
Ugliness

MOTIFS

Veils

Faces
Dreams

SYMBOLS

Door
Dam

TOOLS

Irony
Paradox

As we begin reading, let's remember what Lewis encouraged good readers to do in *An Experiment in Criticism*.

1. Begin reading with an empty mind and good will.

2. Remember who the author is by looking for shared human experiences in their words, but also remember that shared experiences are limited by their humanness.

3. Go beyond the first impression. Study the things and the period around the piece then re-enter the poem or story again.

4. "Find out what the author actually wrote and what the hard words meant and what the allusions were to."

PART I

As you begin Lewis's tale, use each chapter's summary, commentary, and questions as reflection to aid your reading.

Chapter 1
A PARTIAL MEMOIR

"that was the first time I
clearly understood that I am ugly"

OUR CENTRAL CHARACTER Orual begins in retrospective, almost bemoaning the end of her life and yet determined to tell us of her youth. As she clarifies that the gods can do nothing to her now, Orual also accuses them. Like Job, she makes her "complaint," especially against the god of the Grey Mountain, Ungit's son.

We quickly understand that Ungit is indeed Lewis's form for Venus from the original myth. A shapeless black mound in a smoky, dark temple, Ungit and her priest are described as Orual's first cemented fears. According to Orual, Ungit both hates Orual and is terrible in strength, for she requires sacrifice and bloodshed.

Though we aren't given a specific time period, we do know that the ancient country of Glome exists at the time of the Greeklands. Its barbarism and pagan culture are clear.

Let's carefully consider each character as they are introduced in this chapter. Orual is a decrepit old queen at story's beginning, but as narrator, she bluntly states that as the oldest daughter of King Trom, she is different as we see with her hair being "shorn" or shaved off—"the first time I clearly understood that I am ugly" (11).[33] As an old woman, she simply states that she *is* ugly, not that she *was,* as the reader would expect.

Ungit resides in her temple alone in the darkness with nothing but a smoke hole for light in the ceiling. Orual firmly and simply states that "She is a black stone without head or hands or face, and a strong goddess" (4). As a child, Orual describes "the girls who

---

[33] All quotations from Lewis are from *Till We Have Faces* (New York: Harcourt Brace, 1980) and are documented by page number in the text.

are kept in her house, and the presents the brides have to make to her, and how we sometimes, in a bad year, have to cut someone's throat and pour the blood over her" (7). Orual's tutor, the Fox, equates Ungit with the Greek goddess Aphrodite (Venus). The Fox specifically tells the story of how Aphrodite seduces the prince Anchises, tricking him into thinking she was mortal.

Anchises awakens from their bed of love, fully aware that he has been duped into sleeping with an immortal (8). As a child, Orual felt this deceitful behavior was typical of Aphrodite or Ungit. In Greek legend according to Hesiod, Aphrodite was born when Uranus, the father of the gods, was castrated by his son Cronus. Cronus threw the severed genitals into the ocean which began to churn and foam about them. From the *aphros* or "sea foam" arose Aphrodite, and the sea carried her to Cyprus.

Homer calls her a daughter of Zeus and Dione.[34] After her birth, Zeus was afraid that the gods would fight over Aphrodite's hand in marriage so he married her off to the smith god Hephaestus, the steadiest of the gods. He could hardly believe his good luck and used all his skills to make the most lavish jewels for her.

Hephaestus made her a girdle (belt) of finely wrought gold and wove magic into the filigree work, which was not wise of him. When Aphrodite wore her magic girdle, no one could resist her, and she was all too irresistible already. She loved gaiety and glamour and was not at all pleased at being the wife of sooty, hard-working Hephaestus.[35] This is Aphrodite, this is Ungit, and she is most temperamental.

For Orual, the Fox's version only confirms what she thought of the goddess. Most clearly, the account of Anchises foretells the divine to mortal union to come in the story. For Lewis, this is the third time Venus appears in his fiction. In *Perelandra* (1943),

---

[34] *Encyclopedia Mythica, s.v.* "Aphrodite." (2015) https://pantheon.org/articles/a/aphrodite.html
[35] *Ibid.*

Tinidril is Venus or the Eve of the planet. In *The Magician's Nephew* (1955), Venus is the governing goddess.[36]

Redival is Orual's younger sister, a natural beauty with golden curls (5). She dislikes studying and teases and torments the Fox (9). That she instigates pranks against the Fox is no surprise.

As nursemaid and slave, Batta is "a big-boned, fair-haired, hard-handed woman" purchased from traders (5). My students often think she has callused hands, but her cruel nature implies that she hits and slaps to discipline Orual and Redival. Even the name "Batta" seems fitting. She rants and threatens the girls with the idea of an impending stepmother. Batta is ever the evil caretaker herself, who delights in using pain to control others (6), very much like an enforcer.

Hired to instruct a future prince, the Fox, a fellow slave, is from the Greeklands. He is "short and thick-set...He was very bright-eyed, and whatever of his hair and beard was not grey was reddish" (6). Orual delights in describing him as inquisitive and happy regardless of his slave status. She loved him "better than anyone I had yet known" (7).

The question of course is what kind of love it is since Orual has not been truly loved by anyone yet. Perhaps it is already the humble affection, the "warm comfortableness, this satisfaction of being together" that Lewis mentions as an aspect of *storge* love.[37]

The Fox is a skilled tutor who enjoys the beauty of poetry yet regularly proclaims to Orual that such stories are "lies of poets" (8). Yet poetry, perhaps the fanciful and imaginative, is itself a reward for Orual's diligent work in all subjects.

Trom of Glome is practically Batta's mirror image. Often demanding, sometimes raging, he knows nothing of kindness, fatherhood, or leadership. Our first insight is his intentional cruelty

---

[36] Andrew Lazo. "'Time to Prepare a Face': Mythology Comes of Age," *Mythlore: A Journal of J.R.R. Tolkien, C.S. Lewis, Charles Williams, and Mythopoeic Literature* 35, no. 2 (2017): 8.

[37] *The Four Loves* (New York: Harcourt, 1960), 42.

to Orual when Trom says perhaps the Fox "can make her wise; it's about all she'll ever be good for" (7).

From his essay "On Three Ways of Writing for Children," Lewis reveals that it is in "fairy tales, side by side with the terrible figures, we find the immemorial comforters and protectors, the radiant ones."[38] Lewis makes clear that there are characters we must fear or dislike like Trom, yet there is hope if we are to see those who are radiant.

Back in the chapter, Trom reveals to his daughters that he has made a match for himself to the *third* daughter of Caphad. I always wonder why Trom makes this proud announcement. How is the third princess an advantage? Was Lewis simply trying to show us Trom's ignorance, his ineptitude? Nevertheless the marriage moves forward, and King Trom demands that his daughters and others perform a Greek hymn at his wedding under the Fox's tutelage.

The Priest of Ungit is scarcely mentioned in this first chapter, but we do see his effect upon Orual. Inspiring fear, he smelled of animal and human sacrifice (11), wine, and incense, something Orual comes to call "the Ungit smell" (11). His bird mask and the animal skins clothing him present a terrifying figure. Descriptive hints like these are eerily similar to the fear Lewis felt as a child attending the "Anglo-Catholic" church at Belsen. He "feared for his soul," though he little knew why as Orual did.[39]

The Priest is the one who first mentions the idea of veils at the wedding. Trom heartily agrees because he doesn't want his innocent bride to take fright at the ugliness of Orual. Again, the Priest insists on the veils first, that tangible separation and covering. We soon realize that this is a significant symbol for Lewis.

---

[38] in *On Stories and Other Essays on Literature*, ed. Walter Hooper (Orlando: Harcourt, 1982), 39-40.

[39] *Surprised by Joy: The Shape of My Early Life* (New York: Harcourt, 1956), 34.

Unnamed, the third daughter of Caphad is not to be feared as a stereotypical stepmother. Orual describes her as tiny, beautiful, and most importantly, of little consequence. Most notably, she is pictured as "thickly veiled" as Orual (12). Why? What irony is this? Is her beauty to be covered equally as Orual's ugliness? The new stepmother is equally full of fear of the King as Orual is. Thus, it seems beauty is no protection against fear.

By chapter's end, Lewis noticeably refrains from introducing Psyche, the central character of the original myth.

THE FOUR LOVES

Within the characters in this first chapter we see allusions to Lewis's *The Four Loves* (1960), a book many Lewis scholars describe as a formula or a way to see into *Till We Have Faces*. Nancy Enright explains that the story shows us "both the beauty and dangers of human love and, despite the dangers, the enormous power of God's love to transform it."[40]

If we look at the first sentence of the novel, for example, the loves appear absent. Orual no longer fears the gods. She never experienced a sense of worship or spiritual love, *agape,* with them. Nor is there the family affection-love of *storge*, the romantic love of husband and wife in *eros*, or the love of friendship, *philia*. Not yet. As summarized in the Introduction, these loves will continue to provide a foundation to understanding the story.

THOUGHT QUESTIONS

1. What do we truly know about Orual in the first chapter? What is your personal impression of her?

2. What effect does placing the story in an ancient, almost unknown, time have on you, the reader? How could an ancient setting be more effective than a contemporary one?

---

[40] Nancy Enright. "C. S. Lewis's *Till We Have Faces* and the Transformation of Love." *Logos: A Journal of Catholic Thought & Culture* 14, no. 4 (Fall 2011): 93.

3. Compare Orual's relationship with Redival to her relationship with the Fox. How do they intertwine?

4. Why does Lewis describe Orual's impression of the Priest? What is the Priest's effect on her?

MOTIF

How are veils traditionally used in the world we live in? How does that compare to their use in this chapter?

THEME

Which themes from the Preface do you recognize?

Chapter 2
DEATH AND BIRTH

*"in one hour, I passed out of the worst anguish
I had yet suffered into the beginning of all my joys"*

ORUAL CARES FOR her stepmother "more like a sister" (14). Soon pregnant, the new Queen is homesick and lonely, not a figure to be feared. In fact, she quickly admits to Orual that she was afraid of her at first. She appears as one more unloved character for a time until Orual says her stepmother loved her "in her timid way...like a sister," or *storge*. The King is predictably delighted with the pregnancy, boasting about the prince to be born and making faithful sacrifices to Ungit.

Barbarism and superstition abound. All stay awake as the king and queen's child comes into the world for fear the child might "refuse to wake in the world" (14). So too all doors must be kept open, for "the shutting of a door might shut up the mother's womb" (14). Lewis's imagery is both horrific and vital here. He combines the impressions of young Orual with the terrible demands of Ungit amidst a scene of red. From red flaring torches to the suggestion of a womb to the great fire to the spilled blood on the floor, all Orual sees is nightmarish and fearful, for Ungit requires sacrifice.

Even more startling is the King's departure from his dead Queen's room. Orual says he was not in his "red rage" but a pale one, "when he was pale, he was deadly" (15).

As an audience, we are not surprised by the King's reaction. Temperamental as ever, the King is livid with Ungit, and in a literal blind rage, he stabs the slave boy clad in white who dared to bring him wine. More blood is spilled.

The greatest of ironies is that this young boy was likely one of the many bastard sons in the palace that we hear of later. Poor

Trom. He can sire a boy in any illicit relationship, just not a royal one.

In a typical fit, he confronts the Priest, demanding justice of Ungit. The Priest is immovable and threatens Trom with Ungit's judgment while Trom explodes, raving against a plague of girls, lifting Orual by the hair and throwing her across the room. In his rage, Trom yells that the Fox will go to the mines and at one point yells, "Faces, faces, faces," as the rest stare at him. Of course we notice the reference to Lewis's title, but what does he really see? Does the King feels the judgment of others?

Orual knows to mask her pain, and that in itself is telling. Perhaps her self-protective response is a veil too. Orual, and even the Fox, are filled with fear at their separation, but it was not to be. A contingent of men from the neighboring country of Phars arrives, and the Fox's help is needed. No thought of the mines or the King's sentence now. Though it annoys Orual and takes the Fox from her, the King has come to rely on the Fox for reading, calculating, and negotiations. He is ever the wise advisor to the King's ignorant bluster.

From the beginning of this chapter, the Fox has become a father figure for Orual; she calls him "grandfather," and he calls her "daughter." At the very least, Orual shares *storge* or affection with the Fox because they do need each other. Lewis describes affection as a paradox—"It is a Need-love, but what it needs is to give. It is a Gift-love, but it needs to be needed."[41]

Orual's small world is black and white. Her father the King is an abuser and tyrant while the Fox, a slave no less, is caring and instructive. Orual calls him "a true grandfather now" with the birth of Psyche (21).

One more sacrifice perpetuates the images of slaughter—the King burns the dead queen's body (20), and she is no longer mentioned. Notice the lack of Orual's response at her death. Though the queen had been kind and affectionate towards Orual,

---

[41] *The Four Loves*, 42.

Orual doesn't mourn her. I wonder if she even felt the barest *philia*.

Imagery surrounding the infant Psyche is a direct contrast. She is large and healthy unlike her mother, "very fair of skin" (20) and quiet unlike her father. Formally named Istra, she comes to be known by the Greek version Psyche. *Psyche* means soul in Greek, and in Greek myth, Istra is the wife of the god of love, Eros or Cupid.

The idea of the four loves is clear. Remember that *eros* is not mere lust, but a desire for the Beloved that "obliterates the distinction between giving and receiving."[42]

But there is one more possibility. John Dunne asks us to consider a biblical parallel. Could Istra mean Esther? Like Psyche, Esther had two names, Esther and Hadassah (Esther 2:7). Lewis even alludes to the meanings of both. For example, *Hadassah* means myrtle, which might correspond to the scene to come where Psyche receives myrtle branches from the people.[43]

Esther, on the other hand, could share up to three meanings depending on the context. When Orual later describes Psyche's eyes as two stars, this could be a reference to the Persian word meaning *star*. Also *Esther* in Babylonian could represent the theonym for Ishtar, a goddess of love and war. Lastly, in Hebrew, *Esther* means "to hide or conceal." Psyche is later hidden or taken away as Orual is hidden behind a veil.[44] These meanings are all possibilities.

The Fox, though, compares Psyche to Helen of Troy (21) and says she is as beautiful as a goddess. This Greek allusion also implies a layer of foreshadowing because Helen brought division with her beauty. Nevertheless Psyche brought immediate joy to

---

[42] *The Four Loves*, 121, 123.

[43] John Anthony Dunne. "'Nothing Beautiful Hides Its Face': The Hiddenness of Esther in C.S. Lewis' *Till We Have Faces*.'" *Sehnsucht: The C.S. Lewis Journal* 9 (2015): 76.

[44] *Ibid.*, 77-78.

Orual—"I laughed because she was always laughing" (21). It is but one more paradox.

Here, I'm reminded of Lewis's words in his autobiography *Surprised by Joy*. His written reflections from the year before this novel found its form can guide us. Joy is not derived from pleasure, "but even from aesthetic pleasure. It must have the stab, the pang, the inconsolable longing."[45] It is a simple delight and an unquenchable longing at the same time. James Helfers notes that Lewis's first commentary on joy appears as early as 1933 in *The Pilgrim's Regress:*[46]

> "It is distinguished from other longings by two
> things. In the first place, though the sense of want is
> acute and even painful, yet the mere wanting is felt
> to be somehow a delight. …But this desire, even
> when there is no hope of possible satisfaction,
> continues to be prized, and even to be preferred to
> anything else in the world."[47]

For Lewis, the mention of joy implies a spiritual need within us, and of course, for Orual. Psyche was a natural beauty "at every age the beauty proper to that age" and "she made beauty all around her" (22). Lewis would add that it is this "appreciative pleasure" that is "the starting point for our whole experience of beauty."[48]

One other distinctive contrast is to Redival's natural beauty. Here, she is developing as a young woman but her beauty isn't unique. And if Redival is coming of age, then Orual must already be that much older. At the same time, we the readers remember that Orual, Psyche, and the Fox have excluded Redival from their

---

[45] *Surprised by Joy,* 72.

[46] James P. Helfers. "A Time for Joy: The Ancestry and Apologetic Force of C.S. Lewis' Sehnsucht." *Sehnsucht: The C.S. Lewis Journal* 1 (2007): 9.

[47] *The Pilgrim's Regress* (Grand Rapids, MI: Baker, 1958), 7-8.

[48] *The Four Loves,* 20.

philia, a friendship that has grown out of their affection now rooted in their intellectual sharing.[49] For Orual, creation itself is more beautiful in every season because of Psyche's presence.

And now time quickens for Orual. Seasons pass as Psyche matures. Perhaps one of Orual's most revealing passages yet is when she expresses Psyche's effect upon her:

> "I wanted to be a wife so that I could have been her real mother. I wanted to be a boy so that she could be in love with me. I wanted her to be my full sister instead of my half sister. I wanted her to be a slave so that I could set her free and make her rich" (23).

Her comments are striking, even awkward for us to read. Lewis cautions that "Every human love, at its height, has a tendency to claim for itself a divine authority"[50] where it becomes the thing or person we worship. Carla Arnell believes Orual desires to make Psyche's beauty her own, though beauty isn't something to be shared.[51]

In her declaration, we know Orual isn't being literal. The pressing question might be whether this is an absolute unconditional love or a protective, obsessive one akin to idolatry. And of course we wonder how Orual could ever learn to love unselfishly. Maybe the love of the Fox comes too late. Maybe it is not enough when she has been trained in fear through her father.

One clue appears at chapter's end. When the Fox delightedly exclaims that Psyche is prettier than any classic beauty, even Aphrodite, Orual is dismayed. Remember that Aphrodite is Ungit. Ever fearful, Orual is certain that Ungit has heard. It is ironic that the Fox who speaks against the gods compares Psyche to two

---

[49] Enright, "Transformation," 102.

[50] *The Four Loves,* 8.

[51] Carla A. Arnell, "On Beauty, Justice, and the Sublime in C.S. Lewis's *Till We Have Faces," Christianity and Literature* 52, no.1 (Autumn 2002): 28.

Greek gods, for his utterance is a praise. And Orual cannot see that her thoughts towards Psyche are worshipful too.

Two details Lewis includes about Psyche bear greater weight within the plot soon. First, Psyche had a strange, "unchanciest love for all manner of brutes" when she holds a toad. Of all creatures at this point, why would Lewis employ the predictable toad, one that could become a prince? Should we ask if her love could change an ugly brute or if that ugly one is Orual?

Secondly, in her childish imagination, Psyche predicts she will be a "great, great queen, married to the greatest king of all, and he will build me a castle of gold and amber" on the Grey Mountain, a place she is "half in love with" (23). What does Lewis imply by referencing this fantasy?

THOUGHT QUESTIONS

1. Why does Ungit demand so much from her people?

2. If Ungit represents the goddess of love, what is Lewis saying about her type of love? Is there any good?

3. Psyche has unusual parents, one timid and one fiery. Why is this? Does it matter?

4. Describe Orual's relationship with the Fox. What is their love like now?

5. Though early in the story, what are the things Orual longs for in these first two chapters?

6. What does Psyche long for? Why is her longing different from Orual's?

MOTIF

How has Lewis used veils and faces in this chapter?

THEME

How does Lewis use paradox in the story?

Reflect on Lewis's purpose so far.
What does he want us to see and know? What can we relate to?

Chapter 3
SIGNS OF FOREBODING

"gods do not tell"

REDIVAL'S DALLIANCE AND debacle with the young officer Tarin end the perpetual pleasant season. Her shallow e*ros* has an unfortunate consequence. Tarin is castrated and sold off as a slave, and Redival is given no choice. The fact that she must now by the King's command always stay with Orual, Psyche, and the Fox is stifling for all. And once again, in the midst of his threats to everyone, the King attacks Orual by saying, "And you goblin daughter, do what you're good for, you'd best...if you with that face can't frighten the men away, it's a wonder" (26).

How horrid. The King is unwavering in his abuse. At the same time, Lewis continues to deepen our sympathy for Orual and to provoke our own thoughts about faces.

Redival's sneering and jeering continue as Glome declines—poor harvest, no marriage for the King, and not an ally in sight. Ever a tattle-tale, Redival is witness to a pregnant mother who approaches young Psyche and asks for a kiss, a boon, especially "Because she said her baby would be beautiful if I [Psyche] did" (27).

As the account unfolds, Psyche reveals that it has happened before, and oh, how quickly superstition returns. Orual fears that the gods will be jealous once Redival illustrates how people bow and cast dust on themselves before Psyche. The Fox calmly states that "the divine nature is without jealousy," for "those gods—the sorts of gods you (Orual) are always thinking about—are all folly and lies of poets" (28).

The Fox speaks as a Stoic, a man who relies on rationalism. For him, the gods are distant. Worship is impersonal. But for Orual the gods are motivated by a selfish *eros* that festers with unpredictable jealousy. Is it any wonder then that this chapter began with *eros*?

In his commentary on chapter 3, Peter Schakel notes that the God of the Old Testament is also a jealous God who demands whole-hearted love from his people: "It is crucial to recognize that the jealousy of God is inseparable from the love of God."[52] A divided heart will not do. Orual sees the truth of one side of that statement, but she doesn't understand what she is motivated by.

Preying on Orual's paranoia, Redival offers to seek the Priest of Ungit's advice. Orual agrees to send her with a necklace from their mother while Redival commands the Fox to find her a young king for a husband. Redival may have been patronizing the Fox, but here she reveals to us all that he is "the real King of Glome" (29). Yes, Redival is a true manipulative brat, but she is essential as she reports the truth as a witness.

Not surprisingly Glome continues to disintegrate. A short rebellion is incited by our young eunuch Tarin's father along with a group of other lords. The King himself rides out to rout them, and Orual describes unnecessary slaughter as the King and his men do not leave off when they should. This furthers the "disaffection" among the people, and Orual claims that the King is now weaker in their eyes. Schakel adds that Lewis is intentional here. In a pagan world, this rebellion and the land's depletion are spiritual consequences for the "desexing of Tarin."[53] But that's not all.

A second poor harvest is apparent as a ravaging plague appears. The Fox is deathly ill, but Orual must take his place working for the King. Though she gains the King's respect, *almost* like a man, Orual also learns of Glome's dire state.

Here, at what appears to be a tangent, Lewis reveals that the King and his daughters can only marry divine blood from other

---

[52] Peter J. Schakel, *Reason and Imagination in C.S. Lewis: A Study of Till We Have Faces* (Grand Rapids, MI: Eerdmans, 1984), 20.

[53] *Ibid.*, 22.

royal houses, and the nobles are grumbling that the King is without successor. This plot element is lacking in the original myth. How humans can be divine is not explained but instead assumed as part of the ancient culture. Since only the royal families share divinity, could this be a spiritual part of how we as mankind have Christ within us? Could this be a subtle allusion to I Peter 2:9 as we share access to God as the royal priesthood?

In the chapter, it is Psyche who protectively nurses the Fox back to health, and now Orual reminds us of her claim in the first chapter—that the god is against her. She speaks of the "subtlety" of this god as rumors spread of Psyche's ability, "the beautiful princess could cure the fever by her touch" (30). Is this jealousy again? We recognize the power of rumor. Yet it is mixed with some type of faith, for the people believe Psyche can cure.

Sure enough, mobs of sick, smelly people appear outside the palace gates. Orual is once again quick to associate smell with Ungit. As the people demand healing and bread, the King determines that Istra must be sent out to appease the people since so many palace guards are ill.

In one way, Psyche here appears as a living sacrifice, a willing example of compassion. Lewis speaks of her character as Christ-like in his letter to friend Clyde Kilby.[54] Lewis clearly states that Psyche is not a symbol of Christ nor is she to be equated with Him. Watson says she is "like the suffering servant in Isaiah 53."[55]

Charles Huttar would add that Psyche is a type. "To call Psyche a Christ figure in no way denies her humanity. We are dealing not with identity but with typology."[56] This meaning looks for a parallel between a specific person and another one of more universal significance.

---

[54] Clyde S. Kilby, *The Christian World*, 57-58.

[55] Thomas Ramey Watson, "Enlarging Augustinian Systems: C.S. Lewis's *The Great Divorce* and *Till We Have Faces*." *Renascence* 46, no.3 (1994): 175.

[56] Charles Huttar, "What C.S. Lewis Really Did to 'Cupid and Psyche.'" *Sehnsucht: The C.S. Lewis Journal* 3 (2009): 37.

Psyche is dressed as a queen, chapleted and regal. She emerges from the dark palace into the light of day. The people respond as if she's a goddess by kneeling in submission and crying out she's Ungit in the flesh (32). For the length of the hot day, Psyche touches the people, and they touch her until Psyche grows pale and she herself is carried away to a sick bed.

Throughout, the King consistently thinks of himself. When Orual is concerned that these actions will kill Psyche, he reacts with "They'll kill us all if she stops" (32). Neither one thinks of what motivates Psyche to help the people, even if she was forced to remain with them.

As Psyche is feverish, she imagines a gold and amber castle on the edge of the Grey Mountain. She speaks of it frequently and soon grows well. I wonder if it is one of the reasons she recovers. She longs for something greater because she believes in it. It is faith. Psyche is more beautiful now than ever and has lost a measure of childishness as she gained "a new and severer radiance" (33). Once again Lewis refers to the juxtaposition of the terrible and the radiant[57] in the same way he referred to Aslan as both "good and terrible."

Meanwhile, people in Glome both recover and die, yet we don't know whether those Psyche touched are among the living. Ever distrustful and suspicious, Orual carefully mentions that the gods won't ever tell us. That's the way they are. They are not being mysterious but rather intentional by withholding the truth of what happens.

The people continue to leave gifts outside of the palace gates for Psyche, even pigeons which are sacred to Ungit. Orual is worried about Ungit's response, but the Fox assures her that since the Priest is sick, her worries are unfounded. Orual is fearful of Ungit the goddess while the Fox assumes the man the Priest is to be avoided.

---

[57] "On Three Ways of Writing for Children" in *On Stories*, 39.

Interestingly enough, Redival now insists on going to Ungit's temple regularly to make offerings. The Fox and Orual always send a reliable slave with her but simply assume Redival has become pious to acquire a husband and to avoid them for part of every day. When Orual warns Redival not to speak with anyone, Redival tersely responds not to worry—men are just as likely to look at ugly Orual as to look at her since they've all seen Istra now. We clearly hear the sass and jealousy in Redival's bratty voice.

THOUGHT QUESTIONS

1. What does Lewis reveal about Redival in this chapter? Why might she be a needed character?
2. Since the King's family is considered divine, what else could this mean? Remember Lewis's comments about Divine Love in the Introduction. How is this ironic?
3. Is Psyche a realistic character? Should she be?

THEME

Trace the theme of jealousy in this chapter. Note which characters are motivated by it. Are there differences between divine and human jealousy? How does jealousy relate to fear?

Chapter 4

FICKLE LAND, FICKLE PEOPLE

*"the mob had now learned that a
palace door can be opened by banging on it"*

ORUAL WORRIES ABOUT how the people of Glome will
continue to react, fretting about how Ungit might be jealous and
about how the Priest and other men could retaliate because of the
unprompted worship of Psyche. Sure enough, the desperate people
return to the palace gates, demanding food. The King surprisingly
gives in and gives out a portion. When he swears that he cannot do
that again because the fields won't bear, several voices in the
crowd cry out that it's because the King hasn't had a son, "Barren
king makes barren land" (36). Immediately, the King signals to an
archer to shoot the man who spoke. The man is killed, and the mob
flees. But famine has its grip on Glome even in the palace.

Orual is next leaving work with her father in the Pillar Room
when she encounters Redival and Batta entering the palace. We
haven't seen Batta in several chapters, but true to our first
impressions of her, she's as critical and deceitful as ever. Redival
first saucily exclaims, "You needn't come looking for me sister-
jailer...when did you last see the little goddess?" (36). Oh how we
hear the dripping sarcasm!

Redival and Batta describe how they saw Psyche on her own
going through a back lane of the market place. Batta mimics
Psyche picking up her robes as she steps into a house. Orual tries
to placate Redival and Batta by assuring them that Psyche is just
fine since the people were worshipping her a few days before, but
Batta seems insistent on talking, or maybe it's rumor-mongering.
Batta must feel it's her duty to report that the plague is worse and
that the people just might be saying Psyche spread the illness with
her touch. Maybe Batta wants to feel important. Maybe she's the
rumour source.

Orual quickly leaves them and goes to the palace porch, awaiting Psyche's return. At the end of the day, Psyche approaches the palace, seeing Orual, and leads her to Orual's own room. Once there, in a moment of natural submission, Psyche lays her head on Orual's knees and sighs that something must be wrong with her because the people are calling her "the Accursed."

Like her father, Orual reacts immediately with, "Who would dare? We'll have his tongue torn out?" Psyche relates that she had gone into the city alone to visit her old wet-nurse who was sick with the fever, hoping to bring her healing. Her previous sickness has not left her in fear.

All was well until she left that house. Psyche describes how she noticed women pulling their skirts away from her as she passed, how a young boy stared and spat at her, and then most cruelly, how a group of men jeered at her and threw stones, calling her "the Accursed." Psyche had fled but was bewildered by their behavior. She is too young, too innocent to know the fickle and changing nature of the mob.

Orual is filled with anger and retaliation, clearly revealing how she sees the people as lesser than herself and the royal household while Psyche had had no qualms about visiting the poor and sick. As Orual declares the King will hear of this cruel treatment, Psyche admonishes her, saying, "You look just like our father when you say those things." Her comment cuts Orual because it is true. Orual is motivated by an extreme sense of injustice in the same manner her father is—with violence.

But what is the root of this? Is it all because of her father? In his comments on affection, Lewis explains that all of the loves are susceptible to jealousy, but that affection is most threatened by change. It is "the most animal, of the loves; its jealousy is proportionately fierce."[58] And I wonder how pride might trigger that same jealousy.

---

[58] *The Four Loves*, 60.

Lewis describes how a family may turn on one member because they change and become different. If a person becomes a Christian when the family is not or when a member becomes an intellectual when the the family is "low-brow," the family reacts. "It is the reaction to desertion, even to robbery"[59] because someone dared to be different. This may explain the people's reaction to some degree as well as Orual's.

Here, Orual utters perhaps the most revealing symbolic statement possible: "You healed them, and blessed them, and took their filthy disease upon yourself" (39). One moment Psyche helps her people. Six days later she is accused. Reminiscent of Isaiah's prophesies of Christ, Psyche has indeed borne the people's sorrows and griefs as they rejected her.

> He was despised and rejected by men;
> a man of sorrows, and acquainted with grief;
> and as one from whom men hide their faces
> he was despised, and we esteemed him not.

> Surely he has borne our griefs
> and carried our sorrows;
> yet we esteemed him stricken,
> smitten by God, and afflicted.[60]

Not only has she become independent of her sister, but Psyche the Accursed has also become symbolic. She cannot be Christ as Lewis wrote,[61] but she is of royal birth and considered divine by her people. In his key letter to Clyde Kilby, Lewis says,

> "Psyche is an instance of the *anima naturaliter*
> *Christiana* [naturally Christian spirit] making the

---

[59] *Ibid.*, 61.

[60] Isaiah 53:3-4, ESV

[61] see footnote 12

best of the Pagan religion she is brought up in and
thus being guided (but always 'under the cloud',
always in terms of her own imagination or that of
her people) towards the true God. She is in some
ways like Christ not because she is a symbol of Him
but because every good man or woman is like
Christ."[62]

She is the one who comforts her sister Orual who's furious
with the people, and she is the one who discerns a connection
between Orual and their father's anger. What's more, Psyche
presages negative times to come.

Though the sisters enjoy a light meal, they both know some
doom is eminent. Orual describes the enduring plague, drought,
famine, (even bees were dead!), and scavenging lions preying on
dying cattle and sheep. Palace work was more difficult than ever
as King Trom continued to fly into rages as neighboring kings
pressed him with demands he could not fulfill. He verbally and
physically abuses both the Fox and Orual.

As the days pass, the plague lessens, and the palace begins to
recover. We hear that the Priest has recovered twice now from the
plague, and sure enough, he comes to the palace with his own
contingent of guards, almost anticipating a fight. He might be old
and blind, but the fear of Ungit still rests upon him as he enters.

Two temple girls lead him, and their description is significant.
Orual says they are "wooden" with their painted faces and white
wigs. Their bare chests or paps, too, are painted gold, and they say
nothing. As in Chapter 1, Orual speaks of an "Ungit smell" that
invades the room with the mix of incense and smell of old age. It
is a "reek" not an aroma. This is the smell she calls "holy." And in
one sense, it is. It is an odor that is distinctive, setting apart Ungit
and her worship from all others.

---

[62] C.S. Lewis to Clyde S. Kilby, February 10, 1957, in Walter Hooper. *C.S.
Lewis: A Complete Guide to His Life & Works* (San Francisco: HarperCollins,
1996) 253.

THOUGHT QUESTIONS

1. Reflect on the first paragraph. In your own words, write a sentence summarizing Orual's thoughts.

2. What is your impression of Orual now? What has changed in your view of her since the first chapter?

3. Why does Lewis have the Priest return from near-death? What kind of worship or belief might the Priest represent?

4. How are the masks the temple girls wear a type of veil?

THEME

Define justice according to Orual and the King. How does jealousy play a part in justice? How does pride intertwine with both?

Chapter 5

THE PRIEST, THE BRUTE, AND PSYCHE

*"Without the shedding of blood
there is no forgiveness of sins."*[63]

THE SCARECROW OF a Priest begins to speak as soon as the King finishes with his overdone welcome. He announces to the King that he and the elders and nobles convened all night in Ungit's temple to discuss what to say to the King about his failing kingdom and his lack of an heir. The King is understandably and predictably outraged yet fearful of the Priest, whom Orual terms "a vulture" (45). In spite of regular sacrifices to Ungit, the Priest insists that the land is impure.

Schakel acknowledges the Priest's simple cause and effect. The woes have come *because* the land is impure[64] and thus Ungit requires further expiation for any person identified as "the Accursed." As the Priest elaborates upon three separate instances where citizens spoke against or acted against Ungit and Glome, the Priest's intent is clear—Glome must be rid of the Accursed and sacrificed to the Brute.

The King thinks the Brute is but a story of his grandmother's, a myth, but the Priest insists that it has been seen again, specifically on the first night the lions returned. Then, the Priest tells the King that Ungit has been speaking to him in the night about "mortals aping the gods" and stealing their worship. Orual immediately recognizes Redival and Batta's influence at the temple. Only their malicious gossip could do such damage, questioning Psyche's actions in the city.

Here, the Fox interrupts by the King's permission and logically questions the appearance of the Brute, declaring that the

---

[63] Hebrews 9:22, ESV

[64] Schakel, *Reason and Imagination*, 23.

head shepherd simply saw a shadow behind the lion because of his torch. The Priest responds that that is but Greek wisdom from a slave. The Priest makes clear that the worship of Ungit cannot be understood by rationalization.

Instilling more fear, he insists that the Brute could actually be a shadow and could be hunting in the city even now, though he would not touch the divine blood of the King. The people would fear and come against the King, and so the King must make the Great Offering. The King listens and asks how to make this offering.

In a mysterious way, the Priest describes that the Brute is Ungit *or* her son, the god of the mountain. The person chosen as the Great Offering is tied to the Holy Tree on the mountain and left for the Brute. That victim must be perfect, but here the Priest's explanation is cloudy:

> "For, in holy language, a man so offered is said to be
> Ungit's husband, and a woman is said to be the bride
> of Ungit's son. And both are called the Brute's
> supper. And when the Brute is Ungit, it lies with the
> man, and when it is her son it lies with the woman.
> And either way there is a devouring...some say the
> loving and the devouring are all the same
> thing" (49).

Without a doubt, most of my students respond in disgust to these pagan statements. However, Lewis is clearly describing an act of covenant, a moment of unity where something is both taken and given, a moment where the soul of each bonds together. This may not be a marriage covenant, but it is a sacrifice and sexual union in one act.

If we look beyond the pagan shell of this description, then we see how Lewis is shaping a spiritual and Christian parallel. To be one with God, perfect and divine love, requires all we are. "Our natural loves are rivals to the love of God."[65] It is sacrifice, not justice.

The Priest continues as he declares no ordinary man or woman will do. Now the King is worried that his divine blood will be called to account. The Fox interrupts again, pointing out the illogic of all the Priest has described. In quite an astute manner, the Priest responds carefully that a slave who did not resist when captured was unworthy, let alone because as a Greek he demands to see clearly and is unable to understand holy things, "as if the gods were no more than letters written in a book" (50).

Lewis captures a particular sentiment in the Priest's words here—those who think they can logically know the gods and their ways by reading or study, or by some intellectual key, are mistaken. They are limited by their minds.[66]

The Priest instead beautifully illustrates how the gods "dazzle our eyes and flow in and out of one another like eddies on a river, and nothing that is said clearly can be said truly about them" (50). If we think we know them, we don't. He continues, "Holy places are dark places. It is life and strength, not knowledge and words, that we get in them. Holy wisdom is not clear and thin like water, but thick and dark like blood" (50).

Walter Hooper reminds us that Lewis has written of this before in his essay on Christian apologetics. There Lewis writes of thick religions based on mysteries and ecstasies as in Africa.[67] Yet Louis Markos notes that we also see Lewis use the word *thicken* in *The Silver Chair*.[68] Aslan tells Jill that he speaks clearly to her on the mountain: "Here on the mountain, the air is clear and your mind is clear; as you drop down into Narnia, the air will *thicken*.

---

[65] *The Four Loves*, 151.

[66] see C.S. Lewis, "On Six Categories of Thought."

[67] Hooper, *C.S. Lewis: A Complete Guide*, 253.

[68] Louis Markos, *Restoring Beauty: The Good, the True, and the Beautiful in the Writings of C.S. Lewis* (Downers Grove, IL: Biblica Books, 2010), 40-41.

Take great care that it does not confuse your mind."[69] I wonder then if on the mountain, with God, truth is most clear. Later in *The Silver Chair*, it is fascinating that the Witch confuses and *thickens* the minds of Jill, Eustace, and Prince Rillian.

Yes, the Priest sounds quite barbaric, yet there is much truth in his words. Dark is not evil, but rather unknown like a limitless place, a place without light by human understanding. Holy wisdom is weighty with many layers and not easily known. In it is life, the life of the blood. Perhaps now as we consider the Priest's words, we can also read the story with God in lieu of Ungit's name or the gods in general.

Ralph Wood comments that "the priest's call to total bodily sacrifice entails a still deeper kind of wisdom, a truth closer to the gospel than is the Fox's Stoic humanism. Christian wisdom is indeed dark and thick with paradox…How could the infinite God identify his purposes with a humble Semitic tribe? More unthinkable still, how could God become a finite and mortal man in Jesus of Nazareth…These are dense and mysterious realities, not thin and self-evident ideas derived from reason alone."[70]

The Priest proceeds and explains to the King how he and the elders drew lots to determine where the Accursed was within Glome. One by one, he eliminates the common people, the elders, the nobles, and then...the lots fall to the King's house. Trom naturally explodes, ignorantly assuming he's been targeted. What persistent pride! He shouts "Treason!" and calls for Bardia, the captain of the palace guard, venting that all the Priest's guards must be killed. The Priest counters that all of Glome is now in arms surrounding the palace.

I can only imagine how the King feels in that moment, when he learns he is the last to know of what happened in the night. The Priest assures Bardia that he would be fighting against Ungit if he

---

[69] Lewis, *The Silver Chair* (New York, Scholastic, 1995), 27.

[70] Ralph C. Wood, "Doubt about the Goodness of God in C.S. Lewis's *Till We Have Faces.*" *Literature and Theology* (Nashville: Abingdon Press, 2008), 73.

obeys the King's orders. In spite of the King's fussing, Bardia says he will not "fight against powers and spirits" (53) as the King calls him a "Girl!"

Bardia is dismissed, and the King turns to the Priest with his knife as Orual and Psyche stand nearby. Holding his dagger to the Priest's ribs, he threatens to kill the queen wasp.

Orual states that the Priest remains miraculously still, without a hint of fear, threatening to haunt the King if he does die. She is sure of the Priest and his faith and expresses that "the room was full of spirits and the horror of holiness" (54). As he confidently proclaims he remains Ungit's voice, the Priest tells them the lots said "no" when asked if the Accursed was the king. True to his character once again, Trom practically smiles with relief, and Orual is disgusted by his selfish reaction, hoping all along that he could see that Psyche would be targeted.

There is a unique parallel in what the Priest describes. Schakel wonders if the castration of Tarin earlier, the removal of his ability to procreate, had so offended Aphrodite (Ungit) that she acted in natural consequence, resulting in the demand for the King's offspring.[71]

The Priest then identifies the Accursed as Psyche. The King feigns sadness, but Orual goes mad. She weeps and begs and clings to the King's feet while he reacts in anger, kicking at her and shouting more insults, unbelievably likening her to cowards and gods and priests and lions, all at once.

She lies still at this point, hearing the men plan for Psyche's sacrifice and her imprisonment that night. They coldly speak of increasing the number of guards against the fickle "weathercocks" of a people, planning for the sacrifice as if it were some typical event. Overwhelmed by emotion, grief, and physical pain, Orual faints.

---

[71] Schakel, *Reason and Imagination*, 24.

THOUGHT QUESTIONS

1. Why has Lewis pitted the Priest against the Fox? What is he showing us?

2. What does the word expiation mean in this chapter? What does sacrifice mean?

3. What other spiritual parallels do you see?

4. How has Lewis used a myth within a myth?

MOTIF

Note the number of times Orual herself comments on faces.

THEME

What does the jealousy of Ungit show us? What could Lewis's purpose be?

Chapter 6

THE REALITY OF THE BRAVE AND THE BEAUTIFUL

"if the one weren't so brave and the other so beautiful"

ORUAL COMES TO as the Fox and King help her to a seat. Almost apologizing, her father gives her a bit of wine and some advice for taking care of her bruises, admonishing her that women simply cannot get in the way. Orual reflects that he is indeed "a vile and pitiable king" with the smallest amount of shame for beating her and not defending Psyche (57).

When the King then reveals that Psyche will be sacrificed the very next day, Orual is beside herself. The Fox tries to comfort her, saying that this is best, when the King counters and asks the Fox what he would do in all his clever logic. The Fox explains how he would bargain for time, "if he were king and father" (59).

He speaks of a love Trom is ignorant of. It is still part of affection, a gift-love that desires good for the one who is loved: "the instinct desires the good of its object, but not simply; only the good it can itself give."[72] In other words, the Fox's love, though good, is still limited by his humanness, yet his is superior to Trom's. Lewis continues, "A much higher love—a love which desires the good of the object as such, from whatever source that good comes—must step in or tame the instinct before it can make the abdication."[73] Yes, this love appears unselfish, but it is still impure until it meets Divine Love.

Naturally, since Trom is not a true father in the sense of love and care, he argues that the Fox's actions would be extreme— "...your counsel is that I should throw my crown over the roof, sell my country to Phars, and get my throat cut" (60).

---

[72] *The Four Loves*, 65-66.

[73] *Ibid.*

With the greatest sarcasm and disdain, the Fox states, "I had forgotten that your own safety was the thing we must work for at all costs" (60). Miraculously, the King either misses or ignores the Fox's impudence. Orual interjects by appealing to the King's pride, telling him that the people might say he was hiding behind a woman, his own daughter. At this, the King reacts in typical Trom anger, exclaiming that it's no wonder he beat Orual, especially since there was no way he could mar her face. Ever verbally abusive, he rages that Psyche is his, and so he has the right to do with her what he wants. He is suspicious of Orual and cannot believe that she loves her half-sister. Trom has now shown us all there is to his person and personality—temper, cruelty, pride, ignorance, selfishness, and a clear inability to understand the nature of love.

And this illustrates one of Lewis's points. Without the Divine Love working through them, the three natural loves of affection, friendship, and *eros* become corrupted, degenerating into jealousy and hatred. One of his best examples of this is the story of the obsessive mother, Mrs. Fidget.[74] Mrs. Fidget was a doer. She was always "living for her family" though they didn't ask it of her. "They did things for her to help her to do things for them which they didn't want done." Her gift-love to them was manipulative. She never understood that giving was to help the recipient need her no longer. Her death, Lewis writes, was a great relief to her family.

As the King explains that one must die for many, just as in battle, Orual offers herself to the Brute in Psyche's place. The King then leads her to his floor-length mirror in the Pillar Room and states that Ungit has demanded the best in the land, "and you'd give her that" (62).

Manganiello writes that this moment and its later echo is in fact "the whole life of an angry young woman in a paradigmatic

---

[74] *The Four Loves*, 63-66.

mirror scene."[75] Lazo further explains how this scene is a reversal of the Narcissus myth.[76] Unlike Narcissus, Orual is ugly and in no way enamored of herself, not physically at least. Yes, she told us of her appearance in the first chapter, but now the King's behavior is ugly, and it's no wonder that Orual notices her physical pain in the very next sentence.

Since Orual can select how she tells her own story, however, we aren't sure we can always trust her words or perspective. Arnell comments that it is important that other characters throughout the story tell us of her ugliness. We know this from the first scene when her hair and Redival's hair is being sheared. The slave women only lament Redival's golden curls. Later when Psyche was born, the Fox sings over her and praises the infant's beauty while Orual is witness. Arnell tells us this image of "her beloved tutor praising Psyche is imprinted in Orual's mind and haunts her as an image of how inequitably love and affection seem to be distributed based on physical beauty."[77] It is unjust to Orual, an "inequality in the nature of things," to be ugly.

Servants, temple guards, even Redival, are gossiping and relating the news of the sacrifice. Orual marks this, but even more so, she tells of the presence of Ungit as she smells incense and animal sacrifice outside with "the reek of holiness everywhere" (62). The smell remains synonymous with darkness, a darkness that feels like confusion.

Redival rushes forward and gushes about poor Psyche and amazingly says "I didn't mean any harm—it wasn't I," confirming what we already knew from Orual's suspicions. At this, Orual threatens to hang Redival by her thumbs to torture her by a slow fire. Redival is dismayed at Orual's lack of empathy, but Orual

---

[75] Dominic Manganiello, "*Till We Have Faces*: From Idolatry to Revelation." *Mythlore: A Journal of J.R.R. Tolkien, C.S. Lewis, Charles Williams, and Mythopoeic Literature* 23, no.1 (2000): 31, 33.

[76] Lazo, "Time to Prepare a Face," 9.

[77] Arnell, "On Beauty," 26.

knows her shallow sister and knows she is only somewhat chastened, soon to be distracted again by a new bauble or lover.

Now after the King's and Redival's ugly words, Orual again becomes aware of the pain in her side and now her foot, but she hurries as best she can to the room where Psyche is being held. Bardia, captain of the guard himself, is guarding it and will not let Orual enter. He is firm and kind in his refusal to Orual's emotional entreaties. Orual runs away to the King's bedchamber and grabs one of her father's swords, returning to attack Bardia. Without any sign of exertion, Bardia quickly disarms the weak and injured Orual who then collapses, weeping.

Bardia at first responds in perhaps a typical virile way by complementing Orual's swordsmanship and bravery rather than acknowledging her tears. Yet as they talk, and Orual even wishes for death, Bardia tenderly comforts her and explains how he, rather than a common sentry, chose his post. Relenting in spite of the King's commands and Ungit's demands, Bardia allows Orual inside, thoughtfully saying, "I wonder do the gods know what it feels like to be a man" (66).

THOUGHT QUESTIONS

1. Why do the Fox and Orual use reason with the King? Is a man like the King capable of being persuaded by reason?

2. What do we learn about Bardia in this chapter? What could his final statement mean, "I wonder do the gods know what it feels like to be a man"?

3. What do we learn about Redival?

THEME

Discuss the growing concepts of beauty and ugliness.

Do you agree with Lewis's idea of Divine Love?

Chapter 7

LAST MOMENTS

*"As a young man marries a young woman, so shall your
sons marry you; as a bridegroom rejoices over his bride,
so shall your God rejoice over you."*[78]

ORUAL RUSHES IN to embrace Psyche, yet it is Psyche who
comforts Orual, which brings its own measure of pain to Orual's
heart. Isn't she, the elder, the Maia or mother, supposed to comfort
her sister who's about to be sacrificed?

Maia in Greek can mean mother, nurse, or midwife, but in
Greek mythology, Maia is also the oldest and loveliest of the
Pleiades, the seven sisters eventually transformed into stars by
Zeus.[79] This Maia is the mother of Hermes, messenger of the gods,
one who uses language and lyre. While he is said to be protector of
heralds and travelers, he also freely travels between the mortal and
divine worlds, a type of soul guide.

With this in mind, Lewis once again deepens a paradoxical
moment where the most beautiful Psyche or soul calls her most
ugly sister both mother and the loveliest of sisters. Psyche truly
sees who her sister is. This is the strongest metaphor for the
chapter because Psyche is operating in a reality where she is fully
aware of the natural and spiritual planes whereas Orual is limited
to her own selfish mindset. They do not *see* the same way.

Orual also tells us that as she first sees Psyche, the imprint of
the scene is most vivid in her mind—Psyche, a bed, and a lamp. It
is a scene that will repeat itself. Psyche is naturally dismayed to
see Orual's bruises and injuries as Orual quickly recounts what has

---

[78] Isaiah 62:5, ESV

[79] William Smith, ed. *A Dictionary of Greek and Roman Biography and
Mythology.* 1844 (Ann Arbor: University of Michigan, 2005).

happened. Orual calls her father a coward who hides behind a woman in battle while the kingdom is at such a crux.

As they talk, Orual admits to us, the readers, that she is dissatisfied with Psyche's reactions. She is disturbed by Psyche's smile, by the fact that she isn't weeping, by her mimicry of the Fox's mantra, by the fact perhaps that she is not as disturbed by her pending death as Orual is. Psyche encourages Orual to not be rash or think of suicide since they—Orual, the Fox, and Psyche— have been "friends."

That word unhinges Orual further as she cries out, "Oh, your heart is of iron" (69). Orual assumed she herself meant more than affection, more than friendship to her sister. But this is proof of her perverted view of love. Schakel writes, "*Storge* [Affection] should work toward making itself unneeded, but, as a natural love, in itself it has no power to do so."[80] The conversation that follows merely proves the point. With absolute consistency Orual reacts sharply. She wants Psyche to need her, and Psyche does not. It is the same possessive distortion of affection mentioned before.

Again, Psyche bolsters Orual, admonishing her and the Fox to stand like two soldiers in battle, to say goodbye to their father for her though it is but a duty, even to remember Redival by giving her all of her gaudy, costly jewels. Orual reacts strongly against this, but Psyche as the voice of wisdom reminds her that she, Orual, wouldn't want to be Redival.

As Orual weeps, Psyche comforts her with the most disturbing words, "You'll break my heart, and I to be a bride" (70). She reminds Orual of the divine blood that flows through them as royalty, a heritage to be proud of. The words of the apostle Peter echo again as he calls us a royal priesthood, God's special possession,[81] called to be the bride of Christ in John 3.

Psyche is not grieving her death as Orual expected but instead embraces the beauty of her sacrifice, almost as a bride-price. The

---

[80] Schakel, *Reason and Imagination*, 29.

[81] I Peter 2:9, ESV

only moment Psyche weeps is when she expresses how she doubts her faith, the what-if question of whether the Shadowbrute and the sacrifice are real, whether her death would be senseless.

As she finishes crying, Psyche explains how the Priest of Ungit came to her and made things clear. She realizes that the Fox only had a limited view of the world, and Orual concurs. It's as if the Fox understood a city on top of the ground but not the depths beneath it (71). Orual, however, takes a negative stance, asserting that the Fox was too good to believe that the gods were real since they are "viler than the vilest men" (71).

Psyche counters that the gods might be real and that they might not be doing the things we accuse them of as if we don't understand them. Lewis describes a similar blindness in *Letters to Malcolm*. Orual confesses to the readers that this type of talk angers her even more. She selfishly wants Psyche to talk of their love, their grief, over parting because it "seemed to cost her so little" (71). Orual cannot stop herself from being the most negative, yelling that the people want the Brute to murder her.

Psyche calmly responds that she knows she will die, even calling herself a ransom for Glome. How else can she go to the gods or be with a god unless she dies in her humanness? Psyche sees herself as a ransom while Orual sees her as a scapegoat.

Orual again violently and selfishly reacts, asking Psyche how their relationship could mean so little. Orual cannot see what Psyche is describing, yet Psyche is the most realistic. She explains to Orual how their best time on earth has come and gone. What real future do they have as the daughters of the King of Glome?

In utter honesty, Psyche further reveals how she has always longed for death. By this, she means that in the purest and happiest moments of childhood when she, Orual, and the Fox were on the hills far from the palace and city and nearest the Grey Mountain, she felt an invitation to go. The longing came when she was happiest. It was such a strong yearning yet she couldn't identify what it was until now.

This is the same longing, *sehnsucht*, already referred to. It is "an unsatisfied desire which is itself more desirable than any other satisfaction."[82] Remember that Lewis calls it a "stab" or "pang," things that cause pain. But this pain is not senseless. It has a purpose. The object of this longing is joy found in union with God. Psyche knows it is near, yet Orual remains willfully ignorant. She chooses not to listen, not to understand.

Orual bitterly realizes that the sacrifice has already begun. Orual interrupts her narrative and reminds us of why she is writing this book, as an accusation against the gods and also as a confessional against herself. And so, she confesses that she was full of a grudging sin. Orual didn't want Psyche to comfort herself with these words and explanations. Instead she is full of anger and grief. Enright adds that "Orual's Gift-love is so deeply entrenched in her Need-love, impelling her to be the giver to Psyche, that it is corrupted by the intensity of her desire."[83] It is Orual who "feels betrayed by her sister's willingness to leave her."[84]

In the midst of this, Psyche recalls with wonder a beautiful imagination of a gold and amber palace built by the greatest king. She sees herself as perfectly chosen and prepared because any other in Glome would be filled with terror and misery at the prospect.

Much like the longing described in Song of Solomon 2, Psyche is filled with anticipation at meeting her beloved as he calls to her. Full of faith, she has always longed for this home and knows she was meant for this. Lewis's use of *sehnsucht* is clear.

At the same time, many moments in this chapter are reminiscent of Dante's Beatrice. Like Beatrice, Psyche tries to lead Orual to see differently. She desires the best for her and serves as the radiant guide moving toward a divine love, if only Orual would follow.

---

[82] *Surprised by Joy*, 17-18.

[83] Enright, "Transformation," 107.

[84] *Ibid.*

Orual only sees that Psyche doesn't remember her or their sweet times as but a small part of her life. Orual chooses to take offense and lashes out that Psyche never loved her. Bardia interrupts with a knock at the door, and Orual must leave with a last "spoiled embrace," one she singlehandedly ruined.

THOUGHT QUESTIONS

1. Why does Psyche cry?

2. Why do you think Lewis used such a layered name like *Maia*? What effect does using the name have on Orual?

3. How does the Fox see the world differently than the girls do? What did the Priest say was wrong with the Fox's perception?

THEME

How does perception work with faith?

Chapter 8
POMP AND CIRCUMSTANCE

"To love, and lose what we love,
are equally things appointed for our nature."

AS ORUAL LEAVES the prison room, she notes the pains from
the beating by her father, yet Orual is determined to join the
sacrifice procession. Once she learns it is to begin before dawn,
she retires to her room feeling "a great dullness and
heaviness" (77). Though she could eat but little, Orual is put to bed
by her maidservants only to wake a few hours later in excruciating
pain as her eye has swollen shut and her bruised or broken bones
have stiffened. Weeping, her women help her dress.

This is a minor yet significant moment because we learn that
her women love her. Yes, they weep for Psyche, but they also
weep for their mistress who is in pain. One even manages to steal
wine from the King to give to her. Their loyalty and affection is
clear, yet I wonder if Orual is blind to it, and not just in this
moment.

Soon, music is heard, and Orual descends with much help to
the Great Hall. The scene before her is most dramatic. Scores of
guards, nobles, and temple girls gather within while the mob is
without. Orual eerily describes the noble girls who are veiled and
wreathed like a bridal party, her father in his best robes, the Priest
in his full bird mask, the lingering smell of sacrifice, but worst of
all, her glimpse of Psyche. She resembles a temple girl painted
gold and wearing a wig, stiff and practically lifeless. Immediately,
Orual blames the gods, saying that they are killing Psyche after
having stolen her—

> "It was not enough for the gods to kill her; they must
> make her father the murderer. It was not enough to
> take her from me, they must take her three times

over, tear out my heart three times. First her
sentence; then her strange, cold talk last night; and
now this painted and gilded horror to poison my last
sight of her. Ungit had taken the most beautiful thing
that was ever born and made it into an ugly
doll" (80).

Orual never makes it down the stairs to the great hall. She falls
and is carried back to her rooms as the procession leaves. For days
after, she is sick and delusional. Orual blames the gods in her
dreams, for she feels they force her to claim that Psyche is now her
enemy instead of her greatest love.

Paradox and rivalry twist together. Lewis explains, "For most
of us the true rivalry lies between the self and the human Other,
not yet between the human Other and God. It is dangerous to press
upon a man the duty of getting beyond earthly love when his real
difficulty lies in getting so far."[85] In other words, each of us often
live in rivalry with those we love because we are selfish creatures.
We must go outside of ourselves to love others well, and it's even
harder to transcend loving each other to loving God above
everyone else. The first part is Orual's selfish struggle.

Eventually Orual recovers and remembers Psyche had done
her no wrong, yet Orual does begrudge her for spending so much
time speaking about everyone else but herself in their last
moments. This jealousy, this selfishness, does not fade. Orual
doesn't dwell on what had happened to Psyche. She thinks only of
herself.

Outside of her small focus, the rains returned to Glome the
day after the sacrifice, and Orual learns that the Fox and her
women have ever been by her side throughout her sickness—"I
was loved; more than I thought" (83). Love is a rare word for
Orual, so even this mention reveals more of her sensitivity as she
is physically and emotionally weakened. Glome too is on the mend

---

[85] *The Four Loves*, 151.

as the grasses and cattle revive, birds return, and the last of the sickness fades.

But as the Fox relays what Orual has missed, a sourness lingers. He speaks of how her father had become "the darling" of the people since he had put on a good show at Psyche's sacrifice. Orual is not at all surprised and calls him a mountebank, much like a snake-oil salesman. The Fox defends him, saying that Trom's tears could have been as real as anyone's. In other news, the neighboring kingdom of Phars is in a minor civil war over their king's successor, so Glome has nothing to fear politically, but there, the chit-chat stops.

Days later, Orual bluntly asks the Fox if he still feels that Ungit and her legends are but lies of priests and poets. He thinks so, but Orual counters that everything changed after Psyche's sacrifice. Is that not proof that Ungit is real?

The Fox visibly wrestles with his rationalism and the natural order of things. His belief as a Stoic means that he trusts what he can see, what is material. In an emotional scene, the Fox mutters that it is cursed chance or coincidence that reinforces barbarian beliefs that the sacrifice worked. Yet he next explains how chance cannot exist because we are all part of one web. One simple thread, such as an ocean wind, came from miles away at the right time to bring rain to Glome.

Orual is not comforted. What if the King had waited a few days more? The Fox insists that the King's and people's deeds were ignorant and evil, but Psyche wasn't. The Fox wasn't there, but he was told that Psyche remained calm without weeping, even when everyone left. As he describes the scene to Orual, he breaks down in grief and has to leave her— "his love got the better of his philosophy," states Orual (85). How true and real.

The Fox is all logic and level-headed the next day. He reasons that loving and losing love are all part of human nature. Didn't Psyche die with everything she could ever want, even a moment of fame like the Greek heroines Iphigenia or Antigone? In the tales of the Trojan War, Iphigenia was sacrificed to the gods by her father

King Agamemnon in exchange for his fleet's safe passage as they headed to Troy. She died for her country as Psyche was sacrificed for hers. Full of faith, Antigone was known for obeying the gods' laws above men's as she determined to bury her forsaken brother. Her moral call superseded her duty to her uncle or the city's laws.

These famed women had no doubts that the gods were real and active, yet ironically Orual invites the Fox to tell the full tales once again as he finds comfort in the telling. She is thinking of him. The next morning Orual announces that she can be Antigone too, and so she determines to ascend the Grey Mountain to bury what remains of Psyche. She understands only the literal element of the story, not the spiritual.

THOUGHT QUESTIONS

1. What truth can you see about King Trom? Does your view of him change with the careful wording of the Fox's report?

2. What worldviews are the Fox's beliefs similar to today?

3. What does it mean for our love to get the better of our philosophy?

4. What is ironic about Orual's choice to be like Antigone?

MOTIF

Lewis introduces a new motif in this chapter. How does he use dreams?

THEME

When do we see affection in this chapter? Note the type of circumstance surrounding these moments.

Chapter 9

DIFFERENT TRUTHS

"everything was changed"

ORUAL BEGINS TO plan a return to Psyche's place of sacrifice on the mountain. Still regaining her strength, she has eluded her father's demands and has not returned to work in the Pillar room. He has apparently made even more of his love for Psyche and is aggravated by the survival of his "hobgoblin" and "whore" daughters. Orual so desires to see the site and bury Psyche's bones, yet she knows her life is purposeless after this task is done. Hers is a reality of dread and hope, a purgatory Orual describes as "deadness" (89).

One afternoon Orual listlessly walks about the palace grounds when Bardia interrupts her reverie. Acknowledging her grief and hoping to help her, Bardia advises her to train with him in swordfighting. After all, in their quick spat outside of Psyche's room, he saw skill and promise. Orual reluctantly consents and soon passes a half hour of distracting work with "sweat as the kindest creature...far better than philosophy, as a cure for ill thoughts" (91).

After the exercises, Orual accidentally hears an exchange between Bardia and another soldier when Bardia replied, "Why yes, it's a pity about her face. But she's a brave girl and honest. If a man was blind and she weren't the King's daughter, she'd make him a good wife" (92). Oh, how kind and cruel, and Orual ironically terms it "the nearest thing to a love-speech that was ever made me" (92). We know Bardia intended no harm, still once again Orual's ugliness is bluntly acknowledged. Just as any author repeats a description or concept for emphasis, Lewis drives this truth as a mallet hits a spike.

Since Orual finds relief and healing in this physical training, she continues to work with Bardia. We can easily see that they are becoming friends. Lewis considers the love of Friendship rare because we can live without it. It is the least jealous of the loves and is based on mutual respect and understanding.[86] But it is more than companionship. These friends share "some insight or interest or even taste which the others do not share and which, till that moment, each believed to be his own unique treasure (or burden)."[87]

One day, Orual speaks of her need to go to the mountain. Bardia understands and insists on going with her because he can ride and protect her. They plan for one night on the mountain, and Orual teases him that the King won't let him go. In an unusual moment, Bardia explains that he can spin a yarn and that the King is easy to get along with. He is different with the men than with the priest or women. Orual is perplexed because she had not seen this aspect of her father. Maybe only a true friend could point that out.

Six days later, Bardia and Orual leave on his horse in the pre-dawn hours. Orual is wearing a full hooded cloak complete with a veil to hide her face. This is the second time in the story that she wears a veil. We know she doesn't want to be recognized on this secret journey. She also wears her short sword since Bardia cautions her about the wild creatures they could encounter, and she carries an empty urn for Psyche's remains.

They make their way silently through the sleeping city, cross the Shennit river, and head for the mountain road as the clouds break and the sun rises. Filled with momentary dread, Orual describes Ungit's temple as they pass by: like a fat slug, it lies crudely constructed of large stones with a domed thatched roof, resembling an oval egg with constant smoke rising from the flame to Ungit. The priests call it a holy shape and say it is "the egg from which the whole world was hatched or the womb in which the whole world once lay" (94).

---

[86] *The Four Loves*, 74, 78, 82.

[87] *Ibid.*, 83.

But this story, like other ancient ones about the creation of the world, may not be meant to be understood. It simply could be man's attempt to explain what he does not know. Orual does not even try to interpret this statement but is filled with relief and a lightening as they pass into the foothills and wilderness. Bardia chooses to go off of the path where the procession would have led Psyche, and they ascend the steepening slopes.

As they top a ridge and can actually see the mountain in front of them, Orual says "everything changed. And my struggle began" (95). Orual surveys a most colorful landscape of little lakes, valleys, hills, woods, and cliffs that bring delight to her. The joy and longing are there. Yet, she is torn by the grief of her errand and the beauty and hope of the scene before her. "Why does your heart not dance?" she thinks. Can she allow herself this lightening of grief? Can the world outside of the palace truly be so beautiful and full of wonder?

These descriptions are similar to Lewis's words in *Letters to Malcolm*, "that pleasures are shafts of the glory as it strikes our sensibility. As it impinges on our will or our understanding, we give it different names—goodness or truth or the like. But its flash upon our sense and mood is pleasure."[88] Root and Neal explain that these moments of pleasure, of simple wonder at nature or a small goodness that happens to us, are in fact "tiny theophanies" connecting us to God.[89]

We understand that *sehnsucht* is painful as Lewis has described. Como expands the idea, saying the longing is "from a place beyond the senses and kindles a hope that there is Heaven, that Heaven is our home, and that we will return there. It is painful because nothing in this world can satisfy it, no matter how hard we

---

[88] *Letters to Malcolm: Chiefly on Prayer* (New York: Harcourt, Brace & World, Inc., 1964), 88-89.

[89] Jerry Root and Mark Neal, *The Surprising Imagination of C.S. Lewis: An Introduction* (Nashville: Abingdon Press, 2015), 36.

may try to do so; it is sweetly painful because we can intuit its origin and our destiny."[90]

The paradox returns, and it is Orual's second invitation to choose. "Who can feel ugly when the heart meets delight?" (96). Weighing her logic, self-control, and these momentary delights, Orual wrestles with these thoughts as they continue. She affirms that this is a "god-haunted, plague-breeding, decaying, tyrannous world" and she knows not to trust the beauty and light she momentarily enjoys. Assuming the worst, Orual states, "The gods never send us this invitation to delight so readily or so strongly as when they are preparing some new agony. We are their bubbles; they blow us big before they prick us" (97). She clearly steels herself with a measure of self-control as she and Bardia near the final ascent.

Past the tree line now, they see a black valley of stone and scree, "as if the Mountain had sores," they must cross as they face a mouth of rock wall. Dismounting, they head to a lower "saddle" where they can see the lone, leafless tree. Ever filled with dread of the unknown, Orual and Bardia approach. They find the iron belt used to chain Psyche to the tree but no human trace.

Bardia insists only the god, the Shadowbrute, has taken her. Only he could remove her with her clothing and jewels without a trace. Orual feels an emptiness. If there is nothing to bury or remove, what is there to do? She suggests they search for any remnant about the tree, and Bardia soon finds a ruby he knew to be part of Psyche's sandals. Orual is encouraged and wants the search to continue, but Bardia explains that he best do it because to go farther beyond the saddle or rock ridge is to go into the gods' country. Not even priests go so far.

Orual insists she join him, so they collect the horse and carefully ascend the ridge. As they crest it, the formerly hidden sun emerges in brightness and reveals below them an astounding jewel

---

[90] James Como, *C.S. Lewis: A Very Short Introduction* (Oxford: Oxford University Press, 2019), 63.

of a valley—bush and vine bloom, trees flourish, water pools and cascades, the air warm. Their senses are surrounded in this echo of the new Narnia from *The Last Battle*: "a deeper country: every rock and flower and blade of grass looked as if it meant more."[91] Bardia reverently calls the haven "the secret valley of the god" (101). They descend into this Eden. As Orual stops to drink amber water at the first creek, she pushes aside her veil. Hearing Bardia and another voice cry out, she quickly looks up, and in shock, sees Psyche herself across the water.

Orual's movements are no accident. It is in this exact moment *as* the sun shines so brightly, *as* she lowers herself in humility to drink of the god's water, *as* she temporarily moves the veil that Orual both hears and then sees her sister in reality.

THOUGHT QUESTIONS

1. What truth can you see about King Trom? Does your view of him change with the careful wording of the Fox's report?

2. What worldviews are the Fox's beliefs similar to today?

3. What does it mean for our love to get the better of our philosophy?

4. What is ironic about Orual's choice to be like Antigone?

MOTIF

How is the veil as a symbol changing?

THEME

Anyone can see Orual's ugliness on the outside. Maybe now we begin to wonder about our own perceptions. Could Lewis be asking us to examine how we judge others or possibly our own ugliness?

---

[91] *The Last Battle* (New York: Scholastic, 1995), 196.

Chapter 10
JOY AND FAITH

"Have you no wonder?"

CRYING AND LAUGHING, Orual is wild with joy at seeing Psyche. Bardia, however, is frightened beyond belief, assured it is her ghost. Psyche appears different as she is tan and lean and wearing the rags of her dress now. Orual calls her "brightface," for she is laughing, full of joy herself, as she welcomes her Maia.

What is this joy? Lewis writes, "the very nature of Joy makes nonsense of our common distinction between having and wanting. There, to have is to want and to want is to have."[92] For Orual, Psyche has come back from death, and she is now a "radiant one," a "brightface."[93]

As Psyche invites Orual to cross the stream, she commands Bardia to remain, which he does gladly. Though he's unsure if Orual should go, she's insistent, and he responds with something we've heard before: "Of course. It's not with you as with us. You have gods' blood in you. I'll stay here..." Previously, the idea of divine blood was mentioned because the princesses could only marry royalty said to descend from the gods, a completely Greek thought.

Now though, Bardia's fear-filled reaction shows us a deeper meaning. As one of the common people, Bardia expresses the truth he knows—the divine blood is real, and he is full of fear and awe.

Orual fords the mountain stream with Psyche's help, and the sisters joyfully reunite, soon sitting down to partake of a mountain banquet. Psyche describes a handful of mountain berries and water as delicacies fit for the gods while Orual thinks Psyche is playing a

---

[92] *Surprised by Joy*, 166.
[93] "On Stories," 39.

delightful childhood game. Lewis simply writes Orual is pondering, "Is P. mad or am I blind?"[94]

Immediately Orual asks what they should do but Psyche counters with "...be merry! Why should our hearts not dance?" And we recognize the same phrase said by Orual as she ascended the mountain. It's as if Orual were Martha busily planning and doing just as Psyche is Mary, full of eagerness, rest, and delight.[95] Psyche even says, "Solemn Orual, you were always one for plans" (105).

Again, Psyche comforts Orual who begins thinking of all that could have happened to Psyche, and Psyche relates all that has truly happened since the day of sacrifice. Almost like an audience, we see her getting dressed, painted, and drugged like one of the temple girls. It was all like a dream, and interestingly enough, Psyche not only describes seeing Orual at the top of the stairs but also tells her she, Orual, was in a dream practically.

Orual doesn't interrupt, and Psyche offers no interpretation as her story resumes. In this drug-induced state, Psyche recounts how the journey was both brief and yet interminable. As the drugs wear off, she tries to speak in a mumble, and she is drugged again as the procession reaches the tree. Psyche is fastened to the tree with an iron belt and chain as the King weeps and wails. We would assume this is just another show for him, but Psyche insists that he was truly seeing her for the first time. Her words echo the Fox's report, lending even more credibility to the King. I wonder if it took imminent death for the King to really see her.

Finally, the King, priest, and people leave, and Psyche is alone. She describes crying for a time before a number of creatures visit her. First, the lean mountain cattle come and go, then a lynx, yet nothing else. Though she tries to comfort herself with her imagination of the god and his amber palace, Psyche realizes that

---

[94] C.S. Lewis to Katharine Farrer, April 2, 1955, in Hooper, *C.S. Lewis: A Complete Guide*, 249.

[95] Luke 10:38-42, John 11

those longings are absolutely gone. Orual inwardly rejoices and thinks later that this could be one other reason the gods are against her. As Psyche continues, Orual seems to always question the reality of what Psyche is saying. Doubt is a reflex for her.

Then, the weather shifts, and the wind and rains come. Psyche declares that "the gods really are, and that I was bringing the rain" (110). Soon, as the wild wind increases, Psyche exclaims that she saw the West Wind, the god himself. She felt insignificant beside him, and he pulled her out of the iron belt and left her in the secret valley.

Orual is incredulous as Psyche vows and insists her experience was real. Still fearful to a degree and in awe of the god's presence, she hears voices welcome her to *her* house as they call her "the bride of the god." Like the original myth, these voices or spirits bathe, feed, and entertain her in the palace. Psyche feels insufficient next to them and explains that she would be like a dream in contrast to the waking world. That is how a mortal feels next to an immortal. After the evening banquet, her husband would come in the night to her. Hood asks us to consider the truth of this: "Could Orual really be expected to accept from her something which she cannot see for herself?"[96]

Orual is jarred out of her doubt and exclaims, "If this is true, then I've been wrong all my life!" (115). Thus, if the gods are real according to Psyche, her soul, then Orual must see them and this palace. Orual sounds much like Thomas demanding to see Jesus, "Unless I see in his hands the mark of the nails, and place my finger into the mark of the nails, and place my hand into his side, I will never believe."[97] As Orual demands to see the palace. Psyche is horribly crushed because they have been standing on the palace steps the entire time.

---

[96] Gwenyth Hood, "Heroic Orual and the Tasks of Psyche," *Mythlore: A Journal of J.R.R. Tolkien, C.S. Lewis, Charles Williams, and Mythopoeic Literature* 27, no.3 (2009): 58.

[97] John 20:25, ESV

THOUGHT QUESTIONS

1. From the first page of the novel, we have heard of the Grey Mountain. What could ascending it mean?

2. If Bardia is fearful of the gods, does that mean he has faith? Does he believe in them?

3. What does it mean to be "almost awake"?

4. Should Orual accept the entirety of Psyche's story? Could madness be subtle?

THEME

What is the difference between perception and belief? How does this relate to faith?

Chapter 11

THE INVITATION

"For you, it is not there at all"

LEWIS WRITES ABOUT the idea of perception in personal letters to fellow Inkling Owen Barfield and also to his friend Arthur Greeves. Schakel points out that Lewis agreed with Barfield that perception did not work with the five senses alone, but with one's whole being, including "mental habits, memory, imagination, feeling, and…will."[98]

In his letter to Greeves when he was younger, Lewis says "you think that your eyes are windows by which your brain 'sees' the world." Lewis goes on to say that science can't really explain the process of how the eye works. Scientists know the eye's nerve communicates like a telegraph wire to you, yet Lewis questions what is the "Thing" that makes it work.[99]

In other words, why do we and why should we trust what we perceive?

As Chapter 11 begins, Orual tells us this is a most critical moment because her charge against the gods hinges on this stalemate. Arnell calls this the "essential injustice" for Orual.[100] Shocked for different reasons, Psyche and Orual are completely silent. Orual thinks of shutting the door in her mind to prevent something from coming in. Though Orual insists they leave the valley, Psyche assumes she can see the palace and that's why she wants to leave.

They argue. Psyche wants Orual to feel an actual palace wall, and Orual reacts in anger by shaking her by the shoulders. Psyche

---

[98] Owen Barfield, *Saving the Appearances: A Study in Idolatry* (London: Faber and Faber, 1957), 20.

[99] Schakel, *Reason and Imagination*, 40-41.

[100] Arnell, "On Beauty," 28.

demands an explanation. Why did Orual praise the wine and honeycakes she gave if they weren't real? Orual tells us she had only drunk water from Psyche's hands and eaten berries, and yet I can't help but think of the door in her mind she needed to shut. Is it possible that Orual did taste of the fruits of the palace and knew it? If so, she's determined not to tell Psyche or us the truth.

With sudden understanding, Psyche recalls the words of her husband and realizes Orual can not see. And with this statement, Orual declares she "almost came to a full belief" (120). She knows Psyche is certain, and she knows she, Orual, is not. It is a sickening feeling.

One simple parallel to Psyche recognized by many Lewis readers is illustrated by Lucy's experience in *Prince Caspian*:

> Lucy's heart swelled with wonder again—"Her face had changed completely and her eyes shone," when she saw Aslan, yet her eyes filled with tears as Peter and Susan denied his presence. It seems as her siblings had grown older, they were unable to see Aslan clearly. Edmund alone believed Lucy. When Aslan later tells Lucy what to do, she's afraid her siblings won't listen to her.
>
> "Will the others see you too?" said Lucy.
>
> "Certainly not at first," said Aslan. "Later on, it depends."
>
> "But they won't believe me!" said Lucy.
>
> "It doesn't matter."[101]

Orual is filled with both horror and grief at the gulf between them, immediately blaming the gods. Their job must be to cause pain and separation. Wood says Orual does not want to live in the two worlds simultaneously. This other "intersecting world is as numinous and paradoxical as Psyche's palace."[102] Orual cries out,

---

[101] *Prince Caspian* (New York: Scholastic, 1995), 125-127, 143.
[102] Wood, "Doubt," 76.

"It's not right. Oh, Psyche, come back!" She does, and they sit for a few moments as once again Psyche comforts her sister.

Psyche explains that she will beg her husband to help Orual see. But as Psyche mentions him—"my god, my lover, my husband"—Orual is enraged and determines that Psyche must be insane, especially because she has not seen him. Even more so, Orual witnesses the "unspeakable joy" in Psyche's eyes as she speaks of her husband. The love Psyche mentions for her husband is clearly healthy and true. From that transformative love, she wants to give to Orual. It is "that Charity from others which, being Love Himself in them, loves the unlovable."[103] And ironically Orual has forgotten that Psyche was "the beginning of all her joys" (20).

Orual still wants to take her away, but Psyche employs logic and asks her to consider how she looks, telling Orual that she will again ask her husband for help. Orual reacts and yells, "I don't want it!" As observers, we know that Orual is implicitly acknowledging Psyche's reality even if it is painful. She cries out that she hates this darkness, this type of confusion. Maybe it's the pain of stepping from unbelief into faith, but Orual cannot and will not do it.

Orual badgers Psyche, demanding she leave, insulting her as she compares her to a temple girl. Psyche is not swayed and declares, "You must come to me" (125). Issued as both a command and invitation, this is Orual's point of choice. Yes, Orual thinks it is madness, and faith indeed must appear so in the natural. But then, it begins to rain.

Orual offers her cloak as protection for she sees Psyche getting wet. But Psyche patiently discloses that they are inside. Orual then "saw in a flash that I must choose one opinion or the other; and in the same flash knew which I had chosen" (126). She has chosen not to believe and still again tries to reason with Psyche, first offering the approaching winter as an excuse and then

---

[103] *The Four Loves*, 168.

trying to command her as a child. Psyche reiterates that she is a wife who obeys her husband, and Orual grabs her arm, trying to pull her away.

But Psyche is stronger. Physical force cannot sway her. Psyche promises to work on her behalf and tells Orual to leave now that the sun is setting. She gently leads Orual to the river and helps her cross. Orual cannot stop begging, offering to become beggar women together wandering in the world or hiding Psyche in Bardia's house. Ever patient, Psyche maintains she is a wife and is happy and leaves Orual there in the deep twilight.

THOUGHT QUESTIONS

1. Orual shuts her mind to keep something from coming in and later states she doesn't want the help of Psyche's husband. What could this mean?

2. How have choice and free will become part of the story?

3. What does Lewis show us about reason and logic?

THEME

What does seeing have to do with believing?

Chapter 12
TWILIGHT

"I saw"

TWILIGHT REPRESENTS SO much in myth—a moment between light and dark, a moment between realities, but especially a moment between what is real and what is supernatural. I've often thought Lewis considered the twilight of the gods as described in Norse mythology, a cataclysmic moment when the world and many of the gods die before a flood. By employing a time of day latent with otherworldliness, could he be foreshadowing the end of the pagan gods, the plural status existing in the barbarian world of Glome?

In the gray light as the sun set, Orual reunites with Bardia who has been waiting for her. He had prepared a campfire and meal before they lie down for the night. Orual reveals that even as they lay back to back for warmth, Bardia would not have thought of her as a woman because "if you are ugly enough, all men (unless they hate you deeply) soon give up thinking of you as a woman at all" (131). Has she in fact laid down her feminine self here? Orual cannot sleep. She is full of thoughts and worries and the ever-present *riddle*—are the gods real?

What happens next is a critical point in her life. She gets up in the morning twilight, pacing, and makes her way to the amber river for a drink. Since we know Orual is speaking in retrospect, she introduces the idea that the water flowing through the gods' secret valley could have either brought clarity or confusion. It is the gods' water. After she kneels for a drink, she looks up and in the mist can see the most unique structure of Psyche's palace. Orual begins to imagine Psyche lying in the arms of her husband and immediately determines to go to the palace steps and beg forgiveness from both him and Psyche.

What a sudden change in thought! She must believe the god is real then. Yet, in a single moment, Orual confesses next "if what I saw was real" (133). Wood wonders if our natural world is constantly intersected by a "supernatural sphere," one that calls us "to discern the natural world through the lens of transcendence."[104] Does it reach past our senses? Unlike her sister who trusted her glimpse of the West-Wind, doubt creeps in for Orual, and as she stands, the sight of the palace fades away in the mist and fog. Enright believes Orual's glimpse of the palace is "a chance given by the gods (God) to return, in repentance, to her sister."[105]

Orual interrupts her narrative to remind us again of her original complaint against the gods. She asks us, her readers, to pass judgment. Is this in fact a sign from the gods? Why would they use a sign she asks? Isn't a sign just another riddle anyway? Why would the gods think something she saw in the twilight could produce a clearer belief? More than anything, she longs for clarity and directness.

Here, as believers, we understand Orual's conundrum. Don't we share these same moments in our relationship with God, moments of doubt, moments of fleeting conviction, moments where we long for a direct instruction from God Himself? "Just speak to me," we think in frustration.

Another thought is that Lewis's choice of the word *riddle* might parallel Paul's use of the word *mystery* in Ephesians 1. In that passage, Paul is explaining what Christ's sacrifice has brought us. We are chosen by God, adopted, forgiven, and lavished with grace, a grace that "makes known to us the mystery of His will."[106] Most translations use the word *mystery*, but the Complete Jewish Bible overtly translates it to *secret plan*. God's secret plan is made known to us. Could this be the riddle Orual is seeking to solve?

[104] Wood, "Doubt," 76.

[105] Enright, "Transformation," 109.

[106] Ephesians 1:9, ESV

Orual chooses not to reveal any of this to Bardia. This in itself leads us to think she knows what she saw was real. If she had described what she saw to him, Bardia out of fear would have immediately concurred the palace was real based on his superstitious beliefs and fear of the place. Maybe this is why Orual doesn't. Bardia cannot be objective.

They begin the return journey down to Glome. As they progress, Orual determines to tell Bardia the story of what happened, intentionally excluding the moment and truth of seeing the palace. When she asks him what he thinks of all that happened, Bardia insists he is pious and faithful and would never intentionally offend the gods— "I think the less Bardia meddles with the gods, the less they'll meddle with Bardia" (135).

Continuing to lie about the palace, Orual persistently peppers Bardia with questions. She manipulates him, appealing to his bravery and his wise insight and finally draws some opinions out of him. Bardia thinks perhaps the Brute must be ugly or frightful or she wouldn't be forbidden to see him. It's no riddle to him. This just confirms Orual's dark suspicions. She's positive the people would agree. The gods got what they wanted and so relieved Glome of its troubles. Yet, her thoughts grow ever darker: "something, so foul it would not show itself, some holy and sickening thing, ghostly or demonlike or bestial—or all three (there's no telling with gods)—enjoyed her at its will" (137).

Orual thinks of the quickest solution. Kill Psyche, and the issue is resolved. This thought brings tears and more variables. What motivates her to think this way? Glover suggests that Orual is "fighting the demons of self-love, self-righteousness, and self-importance."[107] Lewis says every kind of love carries a mixture. "They carry in them the seeds of hatred. If Affection is made the absolute sovereign of a human life the seeds will germinate. Love,

[107] Donald E. Glover, "The Magician's Book: That's Not Your Story." *Studies in the Literary Imagination* 22, no. 2 (Fall 1989): 223.

having become a god, becomes a demon."[108] Orual has lost the power to control Psyche through her distorted love. Should she interfere? Wasn't Psyche happy?

The questions continue, but Orual has made a decision. Psyche will not be "sport for a demon," and Orual says she would kill her out of love. "I perceived now that there is a love deeper than theirs who seek only the happiness of their beloved" (138). So Orual's view of love twists and perverts even further as she returns to the palace.

THOUGHT QUESTIONS

1. What is Lewis showing us about Bardia? What type of believer or follower is he?

2. What do you think of Lewis's use of the word riddle?

3. How would you answer Orual's questions? "Does [a glimpse of the palace] tell against the gods or against me? If they had an honest intention to guide us, why is their guidance not plain?"

THEME

What has changed in Lewis's treatment of love, specifically affection?

If Psyche might represent the soul or the part of us that does have faith, what is Orual saying? Would we consider "killing" that part of us? Why?

---

[108] *The Four Loves*, 56.

Chapter 13

JUSTIFICATION

"My terrible temptation came back;
to leave her to that fool-happy dream…"

THE FOX WAS waiting, like most foxes do. Orual announces that Psyche is alive and well, and she will tell him everything once she has eaten and dried herself. Here, we also meet Orual's only named slave, Poobi. In my classes, my students always laugh at her name. After a few years of this reaction, I'm now inclined to think Lewis introduces her, or more aptly, her name as comic relief. What humor to introduce a character who cannot speak to us yet whose name causes a giggle or two.

The sweet and sour comes, as Orual calls it. One minute she tells the Fox that Psyche is alive and happy even, the next she reveals the entire story, minus her glimpse of the palace. The Fox is understandably crushed, assured Psyche is mad. Suddenly, Orual introduces the thought that all is not as it appears: "you don't think…there might be things that are real because we don't see them?" (141).

Most of us would assume a discussion of faith is imminent. Instead, we return to the comfortable world of philosophy and logic. The Fox slips into analytical mode and answers Orual first with things we logically can't see, like abstract concepts and things in the dark, even the concept of the human soul. As in the early pages of *Surprised by Joy*, "The Fox reminds us of Lewis rationalizing his own unbelief…This view seeks to explain myth away."[109] But Orual is not sidetracked. She knows what the Fox means by the soul. She wants to know what else could exist.

As they argue further, Orual must know what it is that comes to Psyche in the dark. The Fox logically asserts it must be a man,

---

[109] Quoted in Glover, "The Magician's Book," 223.

specifically a mountain man, outlaw, or vagabond living on the mountain. Orual seems genuinely shocked, yet minutes before she had toyed with telling the Fox what she had really seen, meaning she knows that the god, Psyche's husband, is real. Could she really be surprised by his conclusion?

Convinced by the idea of a mountain man, the Fox reasons through the entire scenario. Yes, a man has freed Psyche, told tales, and led her into a fantasy world. Orual is amazed at how plausible this scenario is just as Bardia's version seemed as real. Oh Orual, how easily you are led, how hard you fight to believe what you truly saw.

The Fox is still perplexed about what to do, how to help Psyche, how to solve the riddle. Lewis uses the word *riddle* again, as if there is something to figure out. But is there? Isn't this further irony when compared to Orual's use of the word?

Meanwhile, the King will be away hunting lions for several days, and Orual is determined to return to the mountain. The Fox again logically states that Psyche will soon be with child as winter approaches. Reacting in utter anger, Orual furiously refutes the thought. A mere man mingle with the divine blood of their house!

Again, the Fox and Orual discuss what to do, whether to hide Psyche or send her away. But the mention here of hiding Psyche in Bardia's house is not minor. Perhaps Orual has ignored the fact that Bardia is married until now. Her reaction to the Fox's comment about Ansit shows us her jealousy. The camaraderie and *philia* Orual and Bardia share now blooms in some small way as Orual's frustrated *eros* for Bardia.[110] True *eros* is unselfish, for it "obliterates between giving and receiving."[111]

As the argument continues, the Fox is sure Psyche would be sacrificed again if the people of Glome saw her. Orual counters that Psyche wouldn't leave anyway. She was too insistent, and

---

110 Schakel, *Reason and Imagination*, 54-55.
111 *The Four Loves*, 123.

they would need force, but Orual must "overrule" her, convince her of "her shame and danger" (147).

Orual continues to rant, and we wonder how she could so quickly set aside the truth. Is she so easily swayed? The Fox wonders the same. He is amazed at her anger, her passions, and especially her declaration that she would rather kill Psyche than leave her to some man. He calms her as only he can: "Daughter, daughter. You are transported beyond all reason and nature. Do you know what it is? There's one part love in your heart, and five parts anger, and seven parts pride" (148). The Fox is so accurate.

Orual continues dramatically, raging about the man forcing or deceiving her, calling him "a runaway slave" or "filth." The Fox takes this personally and responds that he is but the same. Orual calms him, assuring him that he is ten times her father. They next speak of the divine blood of the royal house. Orual is sure the Fox does not believe in it, and in most ways, he does not. He does offer some traditional Stoicism though, stating that the divine is in all men, even the man who has Psyche.

Suddenly, the Fox becomes weary and retires for the night. Orual seems to think he is avoiding the discussion and sees his choice for sleep as a weakness. She's convinced that a woman, or a woman who loves you, would not have done so. Glyer adds that moments like these speak to the authentic female voice Lewis uses. It's the "need to make sense of her experience by talking it through, the need for a companion to stay with her through that process of discovery, the anger, the sense of abandonment, all these aspects and more seem to me to reflect a woman's point of view."[112]

The riddle must be solved. Orual's thoughts and accusations continue to deteriorate once the Fox leaves. "Surely everyone has left me! Surely no one truly cares for Psyche!" She is alone and full of abandonment. She must solve the riddle and will probably

---

[112] Glyer, "Joy Davidman Lewis," 14.

CHRISTINE L. NORVELL

guess wrong, so fatalistically sure is she of the vindictive gods. Wood adds that in Orual's mind

> "…these divinities are cruel, even hideous in the demands they place upon us…Worst of all the gods do not merely *permit* our anguish but actually *cause* it. They win the love of those whom we cherish as our own. Thus are our dearest ones 'stolen' in this precise way: they come to love and trust and obey divinity even more than us. Orual is no mere atheist, therefore, but a bitter anti-theist: she hates and despises these love-robbing gods."[113]

Once she dismisses Poobi to bed, Orual lays prostrate on the floor and prays to the gods by herself. She repents, she vows, she promises, and hears nothing. Feeling she is left alone, Orual determines to do something in the morning. After a short sleep, she acknowledges that both Bardia and the Fox have strong theories. But these theories only exacerbate her dilemma. She calls it being "the child of Glome and a pupil of the Fox" (151). Only, Orual now sees that she knows it is a possibility that the "man" could in fact be good. However she justifies her actions, Orual feels a need to be stern and forcible with her love.

THOUGHT QUESTIONS

1. What is it in Orual that drives her to fix the riddle of Psyche?
2. Summarize Bardia's and the Fox's explanations.

---

[113] Wood, "Doubt," 77.

THEME

What is your answer to Orual's question to the Fox, "you don't think...there might be things that are real because we don't see them?"

Chapter 14

THE CHALLENGE

"Nothing that's beautiful hides its face."

MORNING ARRIVES, THE King has left, and so must Orual. Her packing list is most unique. Again she brings the urn originally intended for Psyche's remains, but now places a lamp, a jar of oil, some linen cloth, and food in it. She eats, then hiding under veil and cloak, departs to find Bardia. Bardia must disappoint her. He cannot be her companion on this second secret mission because he is in charge of the palace while the King is away. He can, however, entrust her to Gram, a small, dark, quiet soldier who is able to ride a horse and accompany her. I wonder at Lewis's dry choice of names again. Does he call Bardia's man a gram because of his size? Or is he a "slight" replacement for Bardia?

Orual asks for a dagger from Bardia, who wonders at her choice, then she leaves to meet Gram. Twice, Lewis hints that Gram fears Orual. Her veil is still on, and we notice that she does not attempt to ameliorate Gram's anxiety. Traveling through rain and wind, Gram and Orual arrive at the secret valley, where light has broken through as it did on the first journey. As an archetype, light often means revelation, that things are made clear. I wonder if that is so for Orual.

Leaving Gram, Orual begins to ford the mountain river and calls out for Psyche who appears immediately. Orual reveals, perhaps in the light of the valley, that they were "two images of love, the happy and the stern—she so young, so brightface, joy in her eye and limbs—I, burdened and resolute, bringing pain in my hand" (157). Yes, Orual can see the contrast and understands it, at least on the surface. She herself says she has no doubt.

Psyche again calls Orual "Maia" or mother, beautiful, reminding her that she would return regardless of the King. I wonder if this could be a return to her own soul (psyche), her own beauty, a true love. Yet Orual shrugs it off and launches into a rehearsed speech about how she is the only one left who loves Psyche and can be trusted to help her, "all the father and mother and kin…and all the King too" (158).

Understandably confused, Psyche assures her that her love for Orual is as strong as ever, even stronger since she has learned to love her husband also. As the god of love, Eros, loves her, Psyche sees love differently than Orual. "Divine Gift-love—Love Himself working in a man…desires what is simply best for the beloved."[114] She speaks of Charity, a deeper, unselfish love, one that doesn't judge.

Orual, however, describes a love that hurts, pulling the thorn out. Lewis also addresses a unique aspect of this jealous love, of any of the loves. He says, "Every human love, at its height, has a tendency to claim for itself a divine authority." It overrides everything else 'for love's sake.'[115] At least that is its justification. Obviously, Orual views Psyche as a child still who needs nursing, who needs guidance from her childish choices. Psyche responds in strength and maturity that her husband will guide her, not Orual. This is the headship Lewis addresses in his chapter on Eros.[116]

Orual thinks that she has the upper hand and pushes Psyche to answer the question as to why the god will not allow his face to be seen. Using "Greek wisdom," Orual follows the traditional rhetorical appeals with logic first. "Think, Psyche," she states, "Nothing that's beautiful hides its face" (160). Orual calls her to think and recognize the facts at the same time stirring her emotions, appealing to pathos. Psyche is still. Why doesn't Orual consider or see her quietness? She reaches for Psyche's hand, and Psyche pushes it away, announcing that she has forgiven her already. Though angry at Orual's accusations about her husband,

---

[114] *The Four Loves*, 164.

[115] *Ibid.*, 8, 58-61.

[116] *Ibid.*, 134-135.

Psyche has calmed herself and asks Orual to put aside these thoughts because she loves her.

Badgering yet, Orual is not swayed and makes an appeal to authority, a certain fallacy, not logic this time. She claims the wisdom and insight of the Fox and Bardia, how both agree Psyche's husband is not who he says he is. Psyche is crushed, "I gave you no leave…it was more like Batta than you" (161). Ah, now Psyche retaliates. Calling Orual a drunken, manipulative gossip should have hurt, but Orual treads on and says all the people of Glome would agree with her, another fallacy normally termed bandwagon. Psyche refutes this, saying that she is his wife, why does it matter to them, why should it matter?

By this point, we the readers feel as if we are in a courtroom witnessing the prosecutor attacking a victim. Orual is relentless, using every bit of ammunition, and Psyche must defend herself. If only Orual was in the audience. She would then see our pity and empathy rise to surround Psyche, not her.

Psyche exclaims that she doesn't have to see her husband: "…how could I not know?" (162). She has been with him intimately, and her love is not based on seeing. She knows he is real, and she knows Orual is limited because she's a virgin. Schakel comments "Orual's virginity, elsewhere a symbol of her barrenness, here symbolizes the limitedness of her experience with love."[117]

Orual doesn't care and demands a test, a challenge—to shine her lamp in the middle of the night and look at the Brute for herself. Psyche insists that the god has expressly forbidden this, yet Orual insults Psyche, calling her a tramp along with Redival, the temple girls, and the King's' lovers. Orual lets her passions rule her logic as the Fox said. Orual thinks it is fear that holds Psyche back from the test, but Psyche corrects her again. Unlike the original myth, Psyche does not operate out of fear or delusion. She would be ashamed to disobey because she loves him.

---

[117] Schakel, *Reason and Imagination*, 50.

Now the sun is setting. Light fades, and so too any hope of understanding. Orual pleads with Psyche to selfishly free her from her fears, and Psyche remains firm that she cannot. At this, Orual dramatically pulls out her dagger and stabs herself through her arm. "Because she knows so little of love, Orual thinks it can be *used*."[118]

Psyche is astounded. Orual calls her to grab the linen in the urn to wrap her wound. We now know that she planned this all along. It wasn't a Plan B but much more. Enright calls it an "act of psychological manipulation that goes against the deepest nature of *philia*."[119] Orual demands a blood oath from Psyche, coercing her. "Psyche prefers to violate the will of the god in pity for her sister, rather than to let Orual die in sure damnation."[120] Psyche clarifies that she is more concerned about Orual's life than her own:

> "You are indeed teaching me about kinds of love I
> did not know. It is like looking into a deep pit. I am
> not sure whether I like your kind better than hatred.
> Oh Orual—to take my love for you, because you
> know it goes down to my very roots and cannot be
> diminished by any newer love, and then to make of
> it a tool, a weapon, a thing of policy and mastery, an
> instrument of torture—I begin to think I never knew
> you. Whatever comes after, something that was
> between us dies here" (165).

Orual does not reflect upon Psyche's words for a second. Ignorant Orual demands Psyche's oath or she will kill them both. Is she incapable of understanding Psyche's meaning then? Psyche further explains that spilling blood on her threshold was the most effective threat. This implies that even in ignorance and in the

---

118 *Ibid.*, 51.

119 Enright, "Transformation," 110.

120 Wood, "Doubt," 77.

shadows of fading light, Orual had managed to stand on the very entrance to the palace she pretends not to see. The irony continues.

Orual holds out the bloody dagger, and Psyche takes the blood oath. But what does Orual's blood accomplish? As in Chapter 2, Orual may only know of blood spilled in anger or sacrifice, just like her father and just like Ungit. And though Orual was granted light in the secret valley, she chose not to see.

But Psyche is able to see this. In addition to the love she will betray, she declares that likely all happiness will be destroyed, all for Orual, "the price you have put upon your life" (166). As Enright expresses, "*Philia* has been unmade between them."[121] Orual weeps and leaves the valley as darkness falls.

THOUGHT QUESTIONS

1. How does Lewis use blood and sacrifice in this chapter? What has Orual sacrificed? What has Psyche sacrificed?

2. How is Orual like her father?

MOTIF

How does Lewis use Orual's veil in this chapter? What about faces? Consider Moses's use of a veil after speaking with God in Exodus 34.

THEME

Compare the love of Orual for Psyche to the love of Psyche for Orual.

---

[121] *Ibid.*, 111.

Chapter 15

AFTERMATH

"You also shall be Psyche."

IT'S TIME TO return to the original myth. In the Greek story, Psyche received her two unnamed sisters at her golden palace on the mountain. Yes, they saw the literal palace. They were awed by its magnificence and the attendants' voices and thus filled with envy, for she had "so much exceeding their own." When they realized that Psyche had never seen her husband, they filled her mind with dark suspicions. Psyche resisted these persuasions for a time, but they did not fail to have their effect, and when her sisters were gone, their words and her own curiosity were too strong for her to resist. Psyche made the choice to disobey her husband in the Greek version out of fear.

In Lewis's tale, Psyche is stronger. She is not tempted to see her husband, but rather feels forced to comply out of love for her sister. She would rather Orual live than die. Lewis's implications about the nature of love continue and cause us to wonder if Psyche's choice was the right one.

Orual rests and waits in the dark on the other side of the river, mulling over the possibilities as she waits to witness a light shine in the palace. She begins with the best case scenario. Psyche would shine the light and then would come across the river, whispering for "Maia!" Orual would dramatically rush out to hold and comfort her, and Psyche would once again love her.

But darker thoughts come too. If the god was real, then she was sending Psyche to her doom, "robbed of all joy" (169). Orual is tempted to right this wrong, but holds herself back, anxious about Psyche's "un-love" for her. Within moments, Orual sees the first light shine and disappear. She retreats to her imagination again as the bitter cold and the pain of her wound make her realize that she could die. Picturing her own funeral, she revels in the thought of Psyche, Bardia, and the Fox mourning her as they express the depth of their love for her.

But the light shines a second time in utter stillness. A golden, great voice cries out in sternness. Full of fear, Orual recognizes in her mortality that it is immortal. After its speech comes Psyche's weeping, and Orual simply states her "heart broke then" (171).

Not only does Orual hear the great voice for herself, but she also sees the great light, a light that reveals a display of power. Lightning strikes repeatedly, felling trees amidst the thunder while the mountains themselves break away in pieces. The river floods, rain batters, and Orual still thinks this is good. She hopes these signs are proof of the rage of some dreadful beast until...

A great light comes. Lewis describes it as a lightning that remains, something that illuminates all, and in its midst was the god, the shape of a man of beauty holding still above Orual. She could only look at his face for a moment, for the divine beauty was too great. In a single look, he rejected her yet "denied, answered, and (worst of all) he knew, all I had thought, done, or been" (173).

Surely he is more than Cupid in the original myth. After all, Orual next says that all her doubt and questions were as nothing before him. In his presence, it's as if she had always known he was real. Wood notes the skill with which Lewis crafts the god. "To have the divinity show his face and actually speak is a virtually impossible task, lest he look and sound like a mere man; yet Lewis magnificently, if also mysteriously, succeeds."[122] This moment brings more questions for Orual because if he is real, then her understanding of her past must change.

The god speaks with both sweetness and intensity "like a bird singing on the branch above a hanged man" (173). I wonder if Orual employs such an image because she knows she deserves to die. Does she think she's about to be executed? Regardless, the god judges them both. He speaks first of Psyche's harsh exile before pronouncing over Orual, "You also shall be Psyche" (174).

---

[122] Wood, "Doubt," 77.

This just might be the greater riddle because the remainder of the novel revolves around that proclamation. Schakel calls it "the gaining of self-knowledge."[123] Then the light and voice vanish, and Orual is left to hear the weeping of Psyche fade away.

The landscape works against Orual, and she is not able to follow Psyche. As dawn arrives, the ravaged valley is visible along with dead sheep and deer. Orual makes her way back to poor Gram, who is more than anxious to depart and says even less than before. Interestingly enough, Orual states that she's "proved" that the gods are real and intent on harming her. She did instigate the debacle with Psyche and Cupid, but she never purposed to prove their reality.

It had all been about rescuing Psyche and regaining her singular love. How Orual's thoughts have changed! As she and Gram descend, the paranoia of impending harm or death increases. Orual mentions falling off a cliff at any moment or turning into a beast the next. The gods are her executioners. And, if she will be Psyche, Orual literally assumes if she survives, then she will be doomed to exile as well.

THOUGHT QUESTIONS

1. Why does Lewis echo Psyche's last moments with Orual from Chapter 7, the scene with the lamp?

2. What does Orual learn about herself once Psyche lights the lamp?

3. What could the god's statement mean "You also shall be Psyche"?

4. Is the god angry?

5. Is the judgment of exile fair?

THEME

How do seeing and believing evolve in this chapter?

---

[123] Schakel, *Reason and Imagination*, 52.

Chapter 16

THE VEIL REMAINS

"A treaty with my ugliness"

SLINKING BACK INTO the palace, like a child who knows they have done wrong, Orual realizes she is avoiding the Fox. Poobi lovingly cares for Orual and her wound, and I wonder if Orual can see her love.

The Fox arrives and is grateful to see her again. Expressing his worry and care for her, he is quite surprised that she had returned to the mountain without telling him. Orual hides her wounded arm and appears ashamed of her manipulation of Psyche. Could she truly realize she had done something wrong? Here, Lewis is careful to describe Orual's shame in the Fox's presence. She is ashamed of what he would think, not of what she had done, not yet.

Eager to hear news of Psyche, the Fox questions Orual. Orual gives a puzzling and circuitous account, beginning with the ravaged state of the valley. She reluctantly admits to speaking with Psyche, but the Fox can tell by her pauses that she is not altogether truthful. Once Orual reveals her plan with the lamp, the Fox is both shocked and distressed. From his viewpoint, the mountain man could have reacted in a number of dangerous ways.

Once again, Orual reflects at how clear his reasoning sounds in the light of day away from the mountain. Yet we know she knows the truth of who the "man" was. And now Orual wishes her veil was on, implying her need to hide from the truth and from the Fox's need for truth. Hood asks us to consider if this is the first suggestion in the story "that her physical ugliness was a symbol for her spiritual ugliness."[124]

---

[124] Hood, "Heroic Orual," 60.

The Fox wants to know how Orual managed to persuade Psyche to leave the mountain, and all Orual will say is that she did. She cannot tell anything further, which saddens the Fox. He knows she is withholding, but he offers her grace and true *philia* again. Part of true *philia* is the openness, the lack of demands put upon friends.[125] The Fox does not pressure or manipulate: "my tormenting you to find it would build a worse barrier between us than your hiding it" (180). Orual weeps at this.

Once the Fox leaves, Orual knows that she will never tell the truth to Bardia either. Amid these resolutions, Orual chooses from this moment on to wear her veil, not as a disguise as on her mountain trips or as something forced on her as at her stepmother's wedding, but as something else.

Her resolution is put to the test within a few days as the King returns from his hunt. Out of sorts as usual, he summons her to the Pillar Room and demands that she remove her "frippery," her "curtains" (181). When she calmly refuses him, the King grows quiet before dismissing her resolve as something all women do.

That small defiance changes their relationship. Orual states "he never struck me, and I never feared him again" (182). At least seeing the god changed that for her. It is the one good thing she brought back. She now demands freedom from tending Redival too, and the King relinquishes Redival's care to Batta. Apparently, Redival and Batta are equal gossips and cheats. Batta has become a strange ally for the king, filling his mind with gossip and flattery.

As time passes, Orual slowly comes to realize that she "might be doomed to live" (183), that the gods might not kill her yet. With that, she goes to Psyche's room and destroys the evidence, burning Psyche's poetry to the god of the mountain and almost anything of her adult life. I'm again reminded of a courtroom scene. In the last chapter, Orual was a badgering prosecutor. Now she behaves like a dirty policeman, covering for herself.

---

[125] *The Four Loves*, 105.

Orual reverts the room and even her memories to Psyche's childhood, keeping only the childish garments and trinkets, a time where Psyche had "belonged" to Orual. The *storge* or affection is frozen. Whereas healthy love grows and changes, the door is locked, and so is Orual's mind to this point in time. The door is used again as a symbol in Chapter 20.

Orual moves on with her life. She demands hard and deeper knowledge from the Fox and fencing lessons from Bardia, determined to "drive all the woman out of me" (184), to ignore the pain she does feel and to fill herself with doing. But Schakel notes that she is working to make herself unfeminine, not just denying her grief over Psyche. "Thus, when Bardia treats her 'more and more like a man,' she is accomplishing her aim; but given the *eros* she feels for Bardia, it is only natural that 'this both grieved and pleased me.'"[126] Lewis also clarifies in a letter to his publisher that "O was in a most perfectly ordinary, jealous, ravenous, biological fashion, in love with Bardia."[127]

At night when she is alone, Orual sometimes weeps for Psyche, wondering at her hardships and exile. And just as quickly she "rebuilds the dam" that she had set in place, the one that keeps her from feeling, the one that perhaps helps her function.

But something unexpected happens. That winter during feast time, the King is injured in a fall on the palace steps. His thigh is broken and cannot be reset. In considerable agony and with considerable alcohol in him, the Second Priest, the surgeon, and the soldiers have difficulty holding him down. In this frantic state, he raves at Orual who is supervising his care. He wants her gone, apprehensively saying he knows who is behind the veil. We know he isn't speaking of Orual. Who else would come and haunt him? The next day is much the same, and it is clear that the King will not recover.

---

[126] Schakel, *Reason and Imagination*, 58.

[127] C.S. Lewis to Jocelyn Green, February 16, 1956 as quoted in Hooper, *C.S. Lewis: A Complete Guide*, 259.

The leaders of Glome—Bardia, the Fox, Orual, and the Second Priest—unofficially convene, and we are more fully introduced to Arnom, Glome's Second Priest. He is the same age as Orual, dark-skinned and shaven. He announces that the Priest is dying, and all there realize the tenuous position of Glome, as both the King and the Priest are failing. Orual thinks the worst and tells us that there will be a new Glome, and that she will be exiled from leadership. These are only her thoughts. Maybe this calms her. She thinks that now she "shall be a Psyche" (186).

Yet within minutes, as the men discuss a needed unity between Ungit and Glome, Bardia declares that there is no issue between the Queen and Ungit. The Fox chimes in, and Arnom is taken aback. What of marriage, what of war? Bardia's quick defense is assuring as Arnom stares at Orual in her veil. Schakel believes her new identity as Queen begins at this moment.[128]

Arnom immediately brings up the single issue that divides them, a fertile river area known as the Crumbles. Orual insists that she speaks for the King and drives a fair bargain, freely giving the Crumbles to Arnom and the temple while retaining command of Ungit's guards.

In an instant, her Queenship has begun, and Bardia whispers "Long live the queen" as the men go to attend the King. Orual, however, does recognize that this newness will not alter the internal barrier she is still building— "It might strengthen the dam, though" (189). Then she realizes that her father will soon be gone.

As the palace quiets for the night, Orual thinks she hears a girl weeping. She follows the sound outside by the well, where she had heard the sound before when the chains moved in the wind. Could the God of the West Wind be stirring them, to draw her to remembrance?

Crying out Psyche's name, Orual waits and hears nothing until she spots a form moving across the grounds. She races after it and

---

[128] *Ibid.*

reaches into the bushes to grab a man's hand as he asks for the King.

THOUGHT QUESTIONS

1. After her mountain experience, why does Orual entertain an alternate theory with the Fox?

2. What is ironic about the Fox's treatment of Orual?

3. Can Orual grieve the loss of Psyche when she doesn't know whether she's dead or alive?

4. What could Lewis's use of a door or dam represent?

MOTIF

How has the veil grown as a symbol?

THEME

How has Orual judged herself?

Chapter 17

THE PRISONER OF PHARS AND THE QUEEN

*"If Orual could vanish altogether into the
Queen, the gods would almost be cheated."*

THROUGH A LIGHT, flirtatious dance of conversation in the
moonlight, Orual meets Trunia of Phars. It's quite the introduction.
One moment she thought she heard her sister, the next, a complete
stranger is telling her how her beautiful voice belies a beautiful
face. It's a brief, harmless flirtation, but it is the second time *eros*
is stirred in Orual until she "comes to her senses." Once again, her
senses, that is reason, reign.

But when Trunia reveals who he is, Orual must play the
politician. She explains to him that she will soon be Queen, and so
calling himself a suppliant, Trunia appeals to her for lodging and
protection.

To remain neutral with Phars, however, Orual cannot help. She
must take him as prisoner, which he naturally refuses. Within
moments, Trunia attempts to run away in the dark, injures his
ankle, and returns to her. She calls for guards who bring him into
the palace where he is fed.

In class conversations, I often stop the story here and ask my
students why Lewis includes Trunia. Some simply say the story at
the moment would become boring without him. Others that Orual
really is a woman in spite of how others treat her in her ugliness.
But of course, why not introduce an immediate challenge to her
leadership?

In the meantime, Orual returns to the King's room. His
condition has worsened but he watches as Orual, the Fox, and
Bardia share news. Trunia's brother Argan and a small force have
entered Glome, looking for his brother. Bardia expresses his worry
until Orual interrupts with her news. Immediately the Queen, she
orders Trunia to be taken to the tower room, where Psyche had

been kept, and Orual and her advisors begin to reason through the sticky situation.

They logically consider several outcomes to a confrontation. The most critical piece of information is that Argan was hated by many and had once done something contemptible and cowardly. Perhaps this is why Orual next asks Bardia what type of swordsman he was. Her thought is that Argan just might agree to fight against one man to bolster his reputation and prevent a battle. Diplomatically, Orual's thinking is most advantageous to her, the country, Trunia himself, and the neighboring kingdom. As readers, I think we are all pleasantly surprised at her deft strategy and self-confidence. We haven't met this Orual, and neither have the Fox or Bardia.

The final stroke of genius comes when Orual announces that the best combatant must be one Argan would be loathe to lose to. The men automatically assume the fighter would be a slave, but Orual counters with herself. We aren't surprised, but the men are. Bardia worries about luck overcoming skill, and the Fox cannot believe a woman could do that, for it was "against all custom—all nature—all modesty" (197).

Within these conversations, harsh truths are revealed. Orual tells us that Bardia doesn't think highly of the "word-weaver" Fox, and the Fox thinks Bardia is a barbarian. But these exchanges also show that Orual's friendship with the Fox has changed. She has withheld her training and intimacy with Bardia from him. Her affection and *philia* are affected by her mistrust.

Yet the men must work together. When Orual argues to fight against Argan herself. Bardia passionately agrees that she could fight and fight well, but states "it's a thousand pities they [the gods] didn't make you a man" (197). What a cruel almost ruinous statement, and Orual's thoughts mirror ours here, as if a gallon of cold water were dashed in your broth. Bardia's declaration almost sounds like something King Trom would say.

And it reintroduces questions about beauty. Arnell asks us if "Lewis presents Orual's ugliness, much like Job's sores and boils, as a seemingly unmerited source of suffering."[129]

To make matters worse, the Fox lowers himself from his lofty, logical soapbox to true emotional appeal. Pathos and tears reign. Women cannot and should not do this. Psyche is gone, and you leave me, an old man, with nothing. He has lost his logic. But, Orual presses the men. Wood says she is now like a "hard-willed king."[130] Like a lawyer once again, she argues that the people would accept her as their ruler if she won. The duel would cement her rule. She forges ahead and states the terms for the fight to be sent by messenger before saying good night.

Alone now, Orual must stop and breathe again. I think even she was surprised by her behavior and quick thinking. She calls that part of her the Queen, but not Orual. Myriad doubts set in —"Where did the bluff and courage come from moments before? What if I fail? What will people think?" But Orual's doubts go further off course in moments.

She next thinks the people might compare her to Psyche if she fails, and within herself, Orual defends and claims a better position, a mental list of her accomplishments, most especially the things Psyche didn't or couldn't do. Orual catches herself of course, thinking she might be a little insane, but it causes us to wonder what is at the root of this competitive stream of thoughts. She is not altogether done. Orual considers whether or not the gods might use this potential fight as a means to kill her, to be rid of her and have their justice.

With that, Orual returns to her father's bedchamber. Terror in his eyes, he is awake but unable to communicate. Orual wonders if he really thought she was Psyche come to murder him. She doesn't delight in his fear but is comforted by the thought that he can no

---

[129] Arnell, "On Beauty," 26.

[130] Wood, "Doubt," 78.

longer control her, alive or dead. Her veil remains, and we wonder when she will use it next.

THOUGHT QUESTIONS

1. Why does Lewis include Trunia as a character?
2. How does Orual describe herself as Queen?
3. Is Orual's ugliness a source of suffering?
4. Why does she think of Psyche at the end of the chapter?

MOTIF

How is the veil a tool?

THEME

Describe what Orual is wrestling with.

Chapter 18

KINGS AND PRIESTS

*"but he holds his priesthood permanently,
because he continues forever"*[131]

THE NEXT MORNING when Orual went to check on the King, she is soon accosted by Redival. Of course, Redival wants to know what will happen to her when the King dies, and at the same time, she must absolutely know who the new handsome man in the house is. Orual is not moved by her emotional banter and severely declares "Your treatment shall be according to your behaviour" (203). Redival immediately reacts by fawning and whining over her sister, hoping for a chance at a husband. It's such a laughable moment, and yet such a quick flash of the new stern Queen.

The Fox arrives next with a genuine apology, "I was wrong to weep and beg and try to force you by your love" (204). His love is not a "fussy show" but is motivated by introspection and charity.[132] Ironically Orual doesn't have a moment to ponder his words. She neither receives nor applies them before Bardia arrives with news of Argan's messenger. After delivering a few insults about having to fight a woman, the messenger relays that Argan will do it, and they take time to lay out the full agreement between the two countries.

The idea of a woman fighting does give us pause, because Lewis has written of it before in *The Lion, The Witch, and the Wardrobe*. There, when Lucy and Susan are given presents, they are forbidden from fighting unless in extreme danger. Markos notes that it's "not because they lack the physical courage or strength but because their presence on the field will make the

---

[131] Hebrews 7:24, ESV

[132] *The Four Loves*, 172-173.

battle an ugly one."[133] He points out that it challenges female and male identities when one role assumes another. Thus, it is even more ironic that Orual's Queenship, a feminine role, is first tested in what is considered a man's role, the duel. It is not Orual's appearance that becomes a thing of beauty but her sword stroke.

The story continues as Arnom enters in full priest regalia, and Orual knows the first Priest has died. Yet seeing Arnom in the bird mask doesn't stir her normal fear reaction of Ungit.

Bardia leads Orual away to discuss both strategy and the reality of killing a man for the first time. Orual is not daunted and even consoles herself, knowing that she was able to stab herself in the arm. Bardia continues and advises her to take part in slaughtering a pig for the day's feast. Apparently, pigs are an abomination to Ungit, but the people may eat them. Orual resolves, "if I shrank from this there would at once be less Queen and more Orual in me" (207). Now we know what she has determined. The part of her that is Orual must diminish, and she is quite conscious of it.

As Queen, she next declares that the Fox is free. Congratulations abound, yet the Fox is stunned after so many years. He must think on it, and suddenly Orual realizes what she has done, "I could not understand the strength of the desire which must be drawing my old master to his own land" (208). She begins to doubt once again, and though she thought the Fox was a "pillar" in her life, Orual is almost sure he will leave her because she had just been his "solace" while imprisoned by her father.

Orual's ramble through numerous untruths continue, but by evening the Fox comes to her, announcing that he will remain because he has been gone from his family and homeland too long. "What would he return to?" he asks. Lewis' physical description of the Fox perhaps says even more. His face is grey, he looks as if he had been tortured, and he even says, "I have won a battle" (210).

---

[133] Markos, *Restoring Beauty*, 32-33.

I'm not sure Orual in her rejoicing truly understood what it took for the Fox to choose to remain in Glome. In her twisted love, she deprives him of what he most desired all these long years—his freedom. Schakel adds that it is not only ironic but "particularly evil—that, having persuaded the Fox to stay, Orual herself later begins to neglect him...Always Orual considers her loves in terms of what they contribute to her, not what she should contribute to them."[134]

That night, Orual is riddled with thoughts, sure that the gods were bringing these great changes. Her awareness of the sorrow she always carried for Psyche had waned, which shocked her. It has always been part of Orual, and she thinks, "Orual dies if she ceases to love Psyche" while the queen side of her is more than happy to let Orual go.

The next day crowds assemble and cheer and the lords and elders arrive to wait with the veiled Queen. Orual goes to Trunia and relates the day's plan without mentioning her part in the fight, and somehow the ever-curious Redival arrives with wine for both, playing her part masterfully. Trunia is sufficiently intrigued, to the point that once Redival departs, he offers marriage first to Orual and then to Redival. Orual can hardly believe the proposal, and we realize it is yet one more event the gods seem to have contrived within this short period of time.

By evening, Orual is practicing her swordsmanship with Bardia, and he is determined to array her in armor fit for a Queen. They go to the King's bedchamber to sift through what armor there is and find the Fox sitting quietly by the King. Moments after they begin foraging, the Fox announces that the King has died. Bardia and Orual pause and yet resume their search, a most pitiful and truthful display of the unimportant life of an unloved king. Is there a lesson to be learned? Both a king and a priest have passed on.

---

[134] Schakel, *Reason and Imagination*, 54.

THOUGHT QUESTIONS

1. Why is Orual no longer afraid of the Priest of Ungit? Is she so different as Queen suddenly?

2. Why did both the first Priest and King Trom die in this chapter? What effect does it have on the story or characters?

MOTIF

How are veils and armor similar?

THEME

Consider the concept of a duel and the meanings associated with the word. What are Orual's "duels" or "dual" roles?

Chapter 19
A KILLING MATTER

*"It was the strangest thing in the world
to look upon him, a man like any other man,
and think that one of us presently would kill the other."*

WHAT DOES A great fight look like? As Queen, Orual soon realizes the preparation is extensive and exasperating. The Fox should appear in formal dress, but he won't. Bardia wants her to go veil-less, but she won't. And Poobi must sew a special veil to fit over the helmet.

Larger than ever, the veil might indeed be "a symbol for symbolism. Like a veil, a symbol conceals in order to reveal: it conceals its meanings behind a literal image in order that they may be conveyed powerfully as they are grasped by the imagination."[135] Ghostlike in appearance, Orual appears daunting according to Bardia. And soon enough, this proves true when Trunia emerged to join the procession. He is startled by her, too.

As the city elders join them, the royal procession leaves the gates of the palace, and Orual does recognize the ironic parallel to Psyche's life. So too, Psyche had left the gates to heal the people and later to appease the people with her sacrifice. Naturally, Orual wonders if this is how she fulfills the god's words. Is this how they will be the same? Will she die in sacrifice?

Maybe we can take a moment here to consider how often Lewis utilizes irony. From the moment of Psyche's birth, itself an irony since she is one more girl, to the fact that the Fox was hired to teach a prince, the tool of irony is quite clear. The Fox never does teach a prince, but he does foster a queen and become a trusted advisor. I'm sure the King never intended it, but he most definitely benefited from it. What other ironies will we see?

---

[135] Schakel, *Reason and Imagination*, 56.

As Orual nears the field, the people stupidly cheer. She knows they are just eager for entertainment. They care not if she wins. Arnom appears in his bird mask, and a sacrifice must be made before the fight. Orual and Argan must each eat a morsel of bull flesh and make the proper vows before the people. The crowds are pushed back, Bardia and Argan's man make the final agreements, and the trumpets sound as the fight begins. Trunia is stunned when he sees Orual remove her cloak and stride out to face Argan while the Fox remains stoic.

Orual quickly measures Argan's disrespect as they begin. To her, the fight was exactly like all of her practice matches with Bardia and appears unchallenging: "I did not believe in the combat at all" (219). Argan soon recognizes how fairly matched they are, and worry sets in. The reality of possible death has arrived. After a second mistake, Orual took her opening and sliced Argan's inner thigh, likely the femoral artery. No ancient surgeon could repair such a wound, and all present know it's a death blow.

Through much cheering, Orual recognizes this death at her hands has already changed her permanently, much like the loss of virginity. Bardia, the Fox, and Trunia surround her with praise, and Orual weeps behind the veil for a moment. But she must address the people and quickly mounts a horse beside Trunia to address the lords and soldiers of Phars. Most of the men shout for Trunia, and the rest gallop away.

Trunia's succession is secure, and she must provide a feast among men when she'd much rather celebrate with an intimate few. Surprisingly, Trunia continues to praise and even flirt with Orual, who very much enjoys the attention and flattery. She realizes that she feels happy for once, but at the same time, knows that the gods won't let it last, "...the gods' old trick; blow the bubble up big before you prick it" (222). But the feminine sympathy does not last either.[136]

---

[136] Glyer, "Joy Davidman Lewis," 14.

Almost immediately word comes that Bardia's wife is in labor, and he is needed at home. Here in a duel, Orual has done the work of a man, bringing death, while Bardia's wife does the work of a woman, bringing life.

Bardia asks Orual for permission to leave, but it's how he asks for permission that disturbs her most, "the day's work is over" (222). Though she maintains her composure in the moment with a blessing to him, Orual is dismayed and discouraged that this powerful and weighty occasion, a crucial moment for her and for Glome, is just work. The stirring jealousy of *eros* is clear.

As Orual hosts the celebratory banquet, she is simultaneously disgusted and pleased by the men's attention. But this is not the place for her. She leaves the drunken mess, but drunk herself, reveals to us one of her strongest imaginations, that of Bardia as her husband and Psyche as her daughter. In one way, we understand that this is how Orual wants to relate to both, yet we know this is her fiction, much like an actor. She feels a "glorious and noble sorrow" for her losses, and her inebriated mind plays a pitiful chorus as she falls asleep with the most final of words, "I am the Queen; I'll kill Orual too" (225).

This connects to Lewis's opening page. Schakel reminds us of Orual's first words: "I *was* Orual the eldest daughter of Trom, King of Glome." Yes, she could be referring to the fact that she tells her life in retrospective, but the past tense could also refer to this moment of choice.

THOUGHT QUESTIONS

1. Why does Orual say, "I am the Queen; I'll kill Orual too"? Did she have to kill a man first to say this, to choose it?

2. How else has Orual become masculine?

3. Why does Orual use the word "lock" again as she did in Chapter 16? (183)

MOTIF

Do you agree with Schakel that the veil is "a symbol of symbolism"?

THEME

What is sacrificed in this chapter? Consider literal, emotional, and spiritual examples.

Chapter 20

A QUEEN'S REIGN

*"And I applied my heart to know wisdom
and to know madness and folly. I perceived that
this also is a striving after wind."*[137]

AND ORUAL ALMOST does know wisdom. She locks part of herself away like a reverse pregnancy, and the Queen part of herself gains dominance. Wood incisively says it's as if she has "performed a spiritual abortion on herself...killing her capacity to produce life, unable to care about anyone but herself."[138] Like her introduction in the first chapter, the Queen remains: "I was Orual the eldest daughter of Trom, King of Glome" (4). Her new identity, though, is her choice. No advisor demands this change.

As years pass, the legend of the Queen evolves. From her fight with Argan to the one battle where she slays seven in a fury to save Bardia, the Queen is famous. In her narrative to us, she is quick to correct and downplay the weave of growing stories. False humility or not, the Queen attributes much of her success to her wise advisors, the Fox and Bardia. Fortunately, neither cares about power and so each gives neutral and balanced advice.

Here, Lewis does say that "they did not think of me as a woman" (228). It does speak to the *philia* they continue to share, but it also means the men see her and love her in a limited way. Lewis's description of male friendship about how men used to plan, hunt, battle, and talk without the women is echoed here.[139] In a sense, both men have helped to diminish her femininity. Bardia had already trained her as a man, a soldier, to ease her mind from the loss of Psyche, yet this treatment somehow remains. Orual

---

[137] Ecclesiastes 1:17, ESV

[138] Wood, "Doubt," 79.

[139] *The Four Loves,* 80-81.

even thinks the gods see women as lesser. By chapter's end, she writes, "The one sin the gods never forgive us is that of being born women" (233).

Her second point is that the veil added to the mystery and the strength of her reign. It sparked incredible rumors. Some said the veil hid an animal face, others an emptiness, and still others dazzling beauty. The Queen even uses it to her benefit in trade and politics to inspire fear and anxiety in the leaders who come to treat with her. She is, as a protagonist, filled with wisdom and courage.

Whatever the veil means to others, Orual still hides herself behind it. Remember that Orual first wore a veil in Chapter 1 as a child because the Priest demanded it at her father's wedding. It is not a wedding veil, a symbol of innocence and parental covering. It is no longer a funeral veil, to hide mourning or to create a separation of privacy. No, these are seasons in life while Orual's veil is permanent.

The question is whether the veil will ever be lifted or removed or by whom. Could there be a veil over Orual's heart too, a natural barrier to block grief or the wounds of being mostly unloved? The Queen next speaks of moving her quarters in the palace to the north to be away from the clanking chains of the well, the ones that remind her of Psyche weeping. But her sister is not forgotten. She admits to employing servants to track every rumor and trace of Psyche to no avail.

What follows in Chapter 20 is indeed a list of accomplishments. Batta is hanged. Slaves are sold off, and some are freed to marry and work the land of Glome, including Poobi. The silver mines are improved upon, the men treated fairly, profit soars. The Fox is given an ample apartment and monies to purchase books, all eighteen in the royal library! The Queen develops relationships with her nobles, and even Bardia's wife Ansit.

Ansit is a typical woman in Glome, no longer beautiful, and quite large after bearing eight children. Our Queen is underwhelmed by what might be in her mind the competition, yet she tries to treat Ansit well. She thinks of all that Ansit shares with Bardia, all the womanly attributes, and then in her mind contrasts those with what she has had with Bardia, all the manly duties. Somehow, the Queen makes herself appear superior. But is that her goal? What exactly is she justifying? Here, I usually remind my students that Orual is the narrator. It is her book and perspective always.

There are improvements in Glome's religion too. Arnom renovates the temple, opening it to light and air, and brings in a new statue that resembles a woman as they do in Greece. Maybe Orual has helped "a coarse, barbaric populace grow into a gracious civilization."[140] The Queen comments that the darkness and holy smell or reek of the temple has dissipated. She admits that "an image of this sort would somehow be a defeat for the old, hungry, faceless Ungit whose terror had been over me in childhood" (234). So, now Ungit has a face in one form and remains shapeless in the other as the two stones stand together in the temple.

In his old age, the Fox writes a history of Glome and begins to call the Queen by more than one boy's name. Perhaps he is thinking of his own brothers or children, those he loved long ago. The Queen continues to fill her hands with doing, and her list begins to sound like Ecclesiastes 2 or the myth of Sisyphus, the story of endless toil, the man who tricked the gods so much he was condemned to eternally roll a boulder up a hill in Hades.

Laws are rewritten, the Shennit river is deepened for trade, water is stored, and so on. She says, "I did and I did and I did—and what does it matter what I did?" (236). It is a conscious busyness that could not fill her as time passes relentlessly.

But Arnell takes it further. She says it is Orual's awareness that her quest for justice was not based on theological values. "By showing her works of justice to be unsatisfying, Lewis affirms a

---

[140] Hood, "Heroic Orual," 43.

traditional theological hierarchy of values," ones anchored by God, ones Orual hasn't been able to truly see.[141]

And so, the Fox dies and is buried, while the Queen's reign slogs on. She finally decides to sojourn to other lands and brings along Bardia's son, Poobi's daughter, and other needed servants and soldiers.

THOUGHT QUESTIONS

1. What changes happen to Ungit's house? Does this suggest a shift in the role of religion in Glome or show us something about Orual?

2. In many ways Glome has changed for the better. Why is Orual not content with her success?

THEME

Read II Corinthians 3:14-15. How could the veil Paul mentions relate to Orual?

[141] Arnell, "On Beauty," 29.

Chapter 21
JOURNEY

"Now, you who read, judge between the gods and me."

THE ONLY REASON Orual even tells us of this journey is because of what happened at the end of it. The trip takes place at harvest season or what we would call early autumn, the end of a season of bounty which is symbolic for Orual. But first, she relates the visit to Phars where Trunia and Redival rule.

Like all women of Glome, Redival is now fat, and true to her nature, ever talkative. Trunia and Orual ignore her and speak together, and we find out that Trunia's second son, Daaran, will assume her throne. Sadly, Orual mentions that she would love Daaran, but she has vowed not to love "any young creature" again, even after all these decades have passed. It is amazing to me that she has lived so long without giving or receiving love, as if love is something dangerous to avoid.

The group then travels through the mountains and forests of Essur, which neighbors Phars. After a brief visit of three days with the King, they journey to a hot springs instead of going home. Lewis spends some time here describing the autumnal season, "...the sunlight on the stubble looked aged and gentle, not fierce like the summer heats. You would think the year was resting, its work done. And I whispered to myself that I too would begin to rest" (239).

Orual's peaceful reflection seems genuine. Her reign is nearing its natural end, the harvest has been gathered, and she feels at rest. In myth and literature, this symbolism of the season is universal and is known as an archetype. Lewis employs it masterfully as Orual's expectations are soon shattered.

As the young ones build camp, Orual wanders into the depths of the cool forest after hearing a temple bell sound. She's drawn to a small white pillared temple in a clearing. All is clean, uncluttered, practically pure, a sure contrast to her prior experiences.

Within the temple, a small two-foot statue of a woman is swathed in black about the face, "much like my own veil," she relates, "but that mine was white" (241). A simple, black-robed priest walks in and greets her as Orual offers a few coins. Within minutes, the priest recounts the tale of this newer goddess Istra. Remember that Psyche too was named Istra at birth and then gradually became known by the Greek name Psyche. Orual isn't fazed by the name as it is apparently common in Essur.

By the priest's tale, Istra was first mortal and was the youngest of three daughters born to a king and queen. As he discloses the full story by memory, Orual is struck by the similarity to her life and interrupts him to ask where he has learned of it. He simply answers that it is the "sacred story" and narrates that the two sisters saw the palace, as in the original myth. This objectivity is crucial. Schakel explains that the priest interrupts the arbitrary nature of Orual's narrative. The outside perspective "authenticates itself—from within itself it supplies the external standard needed to guard against total subjectivity. Thus Lewis's belief in the value of narrative is affirmed."[142]

Orual is stunned. She interrupts and counters that it is not true. He states that "they weren't blind" (243). Donald Glover maintains this is because "Lewis has carefully presented the main plot as a mistaken account of events, pointing toward the human tendency to self-deception. Orual has need to see herself in a kinder light"[143] until now.

Orual's struggle with the gods and her struggle with doubt forcefully re-emerge from the walls she had built. She blusters and fusses and defends her perspective—no fool could have come up with the priest's version. What are the gods up to? She quickly

---

142 Schakel, "Reason and Imagination," 68.

143 Donald E. Glover, "The Magician's Book: That's Not Your Story." *Studies in the Literary Imagination* 22, no. 2 (Fall 1989): 222.

returns to her accusation, "Do I not do well to write a book against them, telling what they have kept hidden?" (243).

If in fact, the sisters had seen the palace, then there would be no riddle and "no guessing wrong." It's as if the defensive veil she wears is being ripped away. The priest said she is not blind, she has seen. "And now to tell my story as if I had had the very sight they had denied me..." (244). Orual's very words reveal so much to us. They denied her. The gods had done this, not her. In her telling, she has removed the choice she had and sounds fatalistic. Schakel argues that this moment is the "middle step between Apuleius's telling and Lewis's retelling, a step needed to show what Apuleius could, perhaps even should, have developed but did not."[144]

But the priest is not done. He next explains how the sisters were jealous of Istra "because they had seen the palace" and all she had (244). Orual explodes again. She realizes she had become like Bardia over the years—leaving the gods alone so that they leave you alone. It had never meant that the gods weren't there or weren't acting. Orual had withdrawn herself, not them. She must write her case against them!

The priest speaks now of Psyche wandering and weeping, of how Talapal (Essur's Ungit) sets difficult tasks for her to complete, of how Psyche is successful and reunited with her husband to become a goddess. To symbolize this momentous change, the black veil on the temple statue is completely removed in the spring and summer. These are descriptions of hope for the doubt-full and antagonistic Orual, but she chooses not to see. She exclaims that the priest "knew nothing" and that the sisters would have more to say before abruptly leaving. But more importantly, Schakel points out, she has interrupted the priest. She "prevented him from completing his sentence with the word *sacrifice*."[145]

---

[144] Schakel, "A Retelling within a Myth Retold: The Priest of Essur and Lewisian Mythopoetics." *Mythlore* 9, no.4 (1983): 10, 12.

[145] *Ibid.*, 11.

Schakel further explains what Lewis is referring to in *Mere Christianity* where "queer stories scattered all through the heathen religions about a god who dies and comes to life again and by his death, has somehow given new life to men."[146] There must be sacrifice, "for it is in sacrifice especially that the old pagan religions anticipate God's fullest revelation of himself and his truths in Christ."[147]

It is now dark, and she makes her way back to the camp, thinking of the feelings she is hiding and of how she must write her accusation, her defense—"I was with book, as a woman is with child" (247).

Though the return journey relays scene after scene of bounty and goodness through Essur and Glome, Orual has removed her inner walls and begins to relive the "terrors, humiliations, struggles, and anguish...letting Orual wake and speak, digging her almost out of a grave, out of the walled well" (247). She urges and forces her companions to quicken their pace and refrains from talking with them. Her sudden and morose behaviour change affects them all.

Once home in Glome (or is it gloom?), Orual is dismayed by the work awaiting her and annoyed that Bardia is ill. She is sure his wife is just keeping him home from her and the palace intentionally. Nevertheless, she finishes her book and finally and clearly spells out her purpose for us in writing:

> "Now, you who read, judge between the gods and me.
> They gave me nothing in the world to love but
> Psyche and then took her from me but that was not
> enough...they would not tell me whether she was the
> bride of a god, or mad, or a brute's or villain's spoil.
> They would give no clear sign...and because I
> guessed wrong they punished me...through
> her" (249).

---

[146] C.S. Lewis, *Mere Christianity* (New York: Macmillan, 1960): 54.

[147] Schakel, "A Retelling," 11.

She has shared these exclusive and limited parts of her life with us. She has told us her story as only she can. And yet Orual calls on us as if we could be neutral as a jury. But can we? Consider her name. The name *Orual* closely resembles the Greek word for *pickaxe*. After reading all that Orual has tried to make sense of, she is still mining, still "picking" for that the valuable gem of truth.

Hood would call us to consider another angle. Our "aged narrator believes that she has awakened the original Orual. This is not really possible, since the years and the task of queenship have transformed her."[148]

At this point, almost all of Orual's theology emerges in the chapter. Orual is sure the gods have created this lying story throughout the world like the one the priest told with the idea that there had never been a riddle, that she had always been able to see, and that she was jealous. According to her, the gods are manipulative and mean and never clear. They give dreams and visions and hints and whispers as if in a game. "Why must holy places be dark places?" (249) she queries once again. Orual ends defiantly—let the gods do what they will, then everyone will know who they are and that they have no answer.

THOUGHT QUESTIONS

1. What is the significance of the setting? What could the bountiful autumn imply, let alone the temple hidden in the forest?

2. Why does Orual ask *us* to judge what is true?

3. What do you think of Hood's idea at the end of the chapter? Even if Orual were to reemerge, is she the same Orual from forty years before?

---

[148] Hood, "Heroic Orual," 62.

MOTIF

How has the veil as a symbol changed? What could the colors mean? What does it mean for the black veil to be removed from the statue of Istra?

THEME

How has Orual changed?

PART II

Chapter 1

A RIP IN THE VEIL

*"Those divine Surgeons had
me tied down and were at work."*

ORUAL FUSSES THAT she must add more to her book even
though she has finished. The writing process itself has taught her
much. What she thought she remembered had awakened even
more "passions and thoughts." More importantly, she tells us she
didn't want to "die perjured." What could this mean?

What's more, "The change which the writing wrought in me
(and of which I did not write) was only a beginning—only to
prepare me for the gods' surgery" (254). What an interesting
phrase! We will soon find out what "gods' surgery" is.

As she wrote the beginning of this very book, something
interrupted her work—an embassy from the Great King arrived at
the palace. The eunuch leader of this entourage was large and
gaudy and yet at the feast she held, Orual knew something was
familiar about him. She suddenly shouted out, "Tarin!" and he
responded that her father may not have loved him but becoming a
eunuch made him a successful man.

Though he repeatedly makes fun of the tiny country of Glome,
Tarin recounts his time with Redival and reveals that Redival felt
lonely and unloved. This is the first time Orual even thinks of how
life might have been for Redival. Before, she only thought of
herself, Psyche, and the Fox. She had always assumed the golden-
haired and pretty Redival had an easier life than herself. This is but
the first small tear in the veil of Orual's defenses.

Orual continues writing and choosing what to write about, so
much so that the process bleeds over into her sleep and her dreams
begin. In her dream, she is endlessly sorting piles of seeds and
grains, as if she could not determine what to include in her book.
Schakel reminds us that the sorting process is "the separation of

what she thought she had been and done and suffered, from what had actually been the case."[149]

In the original myth, Venus gave Psyche this impossible task because it was impossible and to keep her from Cupid, the one she loved. But in the myth, it was no dream, which makes us wonder how it fully applies to Orual's waking life. Remember that the god of the Grey Mountain said, "You also shall be Psyche." And so Lewis has drawn in another parallel from the myth. Yet Orual dreams of this over and over, sometimes dreaming of herself as an ant, vainly trying to lift a single seed when there are thousands.

Her nights and days are full of these thoughts and memories and writing, and somehow she neglects to ask after Bardia until Arnom appears on the very day she finishes. Orual suddenly understands his news that Bardia has been ill for some time and is too weary to fight it. Arnom wisely cautions her not to go to him because then Bardia would feel obligated to rise and be of service. Orual waits in agony. Five days later Bardia dies. Though she knows it would have embarrassed and shamed him, Orual regrets that she never told him she loved him.

Days later at Bardia's funeral pyre, Orual cannot weep or cry out, for only family is allowed to. Her pain is great. She later visits his widow Ansit, who receives her formally while Orual makes a gracious condolence speech. It is a stiff and awkward meeting, yet as the exchange continues, Ansit quickly turns blunt and unforgiving. She reveals that Bardia was not strong but "a tree that is eaten away within" (260). He had been overworked and overloyal for years. Ansit accuses Orual indirectly of overworking Bardia in the Pillar Room, just like any man in the mines.

If only she had known, Orual states. But Ansit plunges on, saying that loyal and loving servants like Bardia surround the Queen. Orual is sure, though, that no one would begrudge her that type of love and loyalty since that is all she has without a husband or children. As her feelings escalate, Ansit lashes out that Orual

---

[149] Schakel, "Reason and Imagination," 70.

left her "her share" of Bardia because he had been so used up by Orual.

Carla Arnell calls this Orual's central discovery because she realizes her "sense of justice has been defective because the love demonstrated to those closest to her was characterized by cupidity rather than charity."[150] This level of selfishness is the ultimate greed, and it reminds me of Lewis's words: "God turns our need of Him into Need-love of Him. What is stranger still is that He creates in us a more than natural receptivity of Charity from our fellow men. Need is so near greed and we are so greedy already that it seems a strange grace."[151]

Orual is stunned and accuses Ansit of being jealous of her. At the same time, she pulls aside her veil as if seeing her ugly visage could persuade Ansit. Instead, Ansit sees the mix of genuine grief and love Orual had for Bardia. This time, Ansit is stunned and brought to tears. They weep together for a brief moment before the argument renews.

Orual wonders why Ansit didn't stop her reliance on Bardia before while Ansit explains that that in itself would have removed Bardia's choice in the matter. To worsen the situation, Orual now has "taken" their firstborn Ilerdia, and Ansit knows she will little see and know him as he serves the palace too.

But perhaps the most grinding and piercing truth comes next. Ansit repudiates Orual for not understanding love. She implies that true love lets go and does not control. Maybe Orual's is unique and not like the rest of mankind: "Perhaps you who spring from the gods love like the gods. Like the Shadowbrute. They say the loving and the devouring are all the same, don't they?" (265).

What? Orual is like the very gods she accuses? What a cruel twist for Ansit to employ these words. She adds that Orual, however, has "fed" and "gorged" herself on the lives of others—Bardia, Ansit, the Fox, Redival, Psyche. Filled with anger, Orual

---

[150] Arnell, "On Beauty," 28.

[151] *The Four Loves*, 165-166.

leaves the room without harming her, though she definitely entertained the idea of torture and death for Ansit.

And now we return to the gods' surgery that Orual first introduced at the beginning of this chapter. I wonder if it is the final "signpost" Lewis mentions in *Surprised by Joy*, where its value is "as a pointer to something other and outer."[152]

The truth of all that Ansit said is laid open before Orual. She cannot deny it or hide any longer. Even her idea of love for Bardia proves empty, "the craving for Bardia was ended" (267). Metaphor though it is, the gods have made the incision and are probing her, causing her to look at herself instead of others. Her bookwriting, her dreams, and Ansit's words have been their instruments.

THOUGHT QUESTIONS

1. Describe how writing helps Orual better understand herself.

2. If Orual has perjured herself, is Part I untrue?

3. Some Lewis scholars see Tarin and Ansit as mirrors. What do you think of this idea? What do we learn of love from Tarin? From Ansit?

MOTIF AND THEME

The dream motif imbues this chapter. How is Lewis shaping Orual's perceptions and our own? What is most real? Or better yet, what is most true?

---

[152] *Surprised by Joy*, 238.

Chapter 2

WHAT VEIL?

*"The voice of the god had not
changed in all those years, but I had"*

IT IS SPRINGTIME, and Glome celebrates the new year. The Priest remains in Ungit's temple overnight before bursting forth and symbolically fighting with someone as a sign that the new year has departed from the West to emerge in the East. In literature, the West is often an archetype for death or winter while the East represents life and spring.

As a virgin still, Orual was not allowed to be part of the overnight rituals as a King would be. Lewis describes drinking, sacrifice, and intercourse with the temple girls. Orual, however, arrives in the morning in the temple with the same lifelong visceral reaction to its smells and "smothering" (269).

As she sits in her designated spot by the original Ungit, she reflects on all the seed that had been spilled and wasted on these temple girls in service of Ungit. All that had been "given" to Ungit was fruitless and wasted, much like Orual's own life of accomplishments. She stares at the shapeless blob and indeed sees faces in spite of the fact that the rock appeared faceless. Again, another irony considering the title of the book.

Orual asks Arnom, "Who is Ungit?" (270). This time, rather than a circuitous answer as the first Priest would have offered, Arnom replies in a rather general way: "She signifies the earth, which is the womb and mother of all living things" (270). She sounds like a caregiver, a nurturer, not the frightening thing Orual has experienced. What's even more interesting is that Orual had just recounted for us, her audience, the original, more primitive story right before inquiring of Arnom. She tells us, the stone of Ungit had not fallen from the sky, but had pushed up from the earth. That statement will help us understand Orual's imminent dreams.

As Orual questions Arnom about what Ungit has made, his answers simply beg more questions. She's convinced the riddle of the gods remains. Who can understand?

A penitent old woman comes in to offer a pigeon as sacrifice. Once the blood is spilled over the stone, she weeps prostrate for awhile but then rises calmly. Orual asks her why she sacrifices to the large stone rather than the new, womanlike statue, and the woman explains that the Greek type statue is only for learned and high-ranking people. The amorphous stone is much simpler and understands her. What does Lewis mean here? Is the old better than the new?

The spring ritual continues, and Orual is amazed by the ignorant joy of the people as they witness this sham fight with Arnom emerging from the temple. Orual soon returns to the palace to rest in her quarters when she is startled by her father's voice. Lewis doesn't clarify if Orual laid down or even fell asleep. Could it be a waking vision?

The King commands her to rise and follow him to the Pillar Room without the veil, "None of that folly" (274), and she does. Her self-imposed barrier is gone. Schakel says Orual must "get beyond her past" by going through it first.[153] Orual is fearful that the King will want his treasured mirror she had given to Redival— or maybe she would be fearful to stand in front of it now without her veil after all these years. They suddenly find two pickaxes (remember her name meaning) and a crowbar in the corner of the Pillar Room and get to work removing a portion of the floor at the King's direction.

Soon enough, a sizable hole is made, and they jump down and fall into a second, smaller Pillar Room made of earth. It's not claustrophobic yet, and we are reminded of Ungit's emergence from the womb of the earth although they are going deeper, deeper

---

[153] Schakel, *Reason and Imagination*, 74.

into herself. The King finds two spades in the corner and commands Orual to dig again. It is harder this time as they dig out blocks of clay, but they make a hole and the King commands her to jump with him again. Though she resists, the King shouts that the Fox and his thinking can't reach her here. Isn't that true of a dream? Our thinking cannot get in the way of the experience or truth of the dream itself. And of course, rationalization is of no help here.

They land in an even smaller Pillar Room made of "living rock" and the roof begins to close in on them. Orual grows alarmed and claustrophobic. She uses the word "smothering" again as she did when describing the sensation that arises when she enters Ungit's temple. The King then demands, "Who is Ungit?" and leads her down a hallway to the mirror. Didn't she just ask that same question of Arnom? This is "a key confrontation in Orual's mind between the rational and the holy."[154]

Orual resists, but for the second time he stands her in front of it. She sees the King's reflection and then her own, which is now the blob of face from the stone in the temple. Lazo sees this moment as a "chiastic mirror image of beauty and ugliness" repeating the moment not only from Book I, but also from Eustace's experience in *The Voyage of the Dawn Treader*. Orual "despairs of her own self-imposed ugliness."[155] The King asks her again, and Orual wails, "I am Ungit!" (276) and immediately wakens. I think it might be the first step in her repentance.

Orual knows it is true, for she had devoured people as Ansit said, "womblike, yet barren" (276). In that instant of recognition, her instinct is to draw her old sword from the wall and kill herself, yet Orual does not have the strength. She feels sure that there must "be something great in the mortal soul" because her suffering, man's suffering, seems unending (277).

---

154 *Ibid.*, 72.

155 Lazo, "Time to Prepare a Face," 9.

That night, once the palace is sleeping, Orual puts on her cloak and removed her veil to walk through the city. She knows now that the veil cannot keep her hidden, for all people know the veiled Queen: "My disguise now would be to go bareface" (278). Many readers will recognize the word as Lewis's first choice for the title of the novel. Manganiello clarifies that Lewis might be referring to a part of George MacDonald's *Lilith* where the apparitions are described:

> "Had they used their faces, not for communication,
> not to utter thought and feeling, not to share
> existence with their neighbors, but to appear what
> they wished to appear, and conceal what they were?
> And, having made their faces masks, were they
> therefore deprived of these masks, and condemned
> to go without faces until they repented?"[156]

Manganiello believes that Orual, like these spirits, must go without a face until she is repentant.[157] We might remember the echo of Orual's words too from Chapter 14 where she said to Psyche that "Nothing that's beautiful hides its face. Nothing that's honest hides its name...in your heart you must see truth."

It is now, in her old and wrinkled body, Orual is unafraid to be seen. She tells us that she is Ungit in all her ugliness, she is holy now. Yet, the irony remains that she is walking about in the dark when no one is looking at her, symbolism in itself. Is she still walking in the dark here at the end of life? She has lived a life of doubt, fearing to believe in something she can't see. I wonder if Orual is still thinking literally since she has removed her veil and even mentions going out naked.

Though she wearies quickly, Orual makes her way to a high bank of the Shennit River, intending to drown herself. She

---

[156] Quoted in Manganiello, "From Idolatry," 42.
[157] *Ibid.*, 37.

removes her girdle, which is a cloth belt, and uses it to tie her ankles together. When she hops almost to the edge, Orual hears a voice cry out, "Do not do it" (279). It is the voice of a god, one she knows, one she has heard from across a river before at the top of the Grey Mountain. Like Saul on his way to Damascus, she exclaims, "Lord, who are you?" (279). He responds that she cannot escape Ungit (or is it being Ungit?) through death. Instead, the god's voice says "Die before you die" (279).

Not only does Orual immediately acknowledge he is who he is by calling him "Lord," but she also knows she has changed within. "No rebel" is left. Manganiello maintains that "Orual's receptiveness to the speech of the god allows him to correct her defective vision" as the story unfolds.[158]

What of the words that echo Christ's? To die before you die. In the gospels, Jesus repeatedly speaks of laying down his life for his sheep, a choice he makes before he is ever crucified. At the same time, he admonishes his disciples to deny themselves, their selfish human natures, and to take up their crosses, their burdens, as they follow Jesus.[159] Isn't this the denial and death of our inner nature? When Jesus encouraged Mary and Martha that Lazarus would rise again, he said, *I am the resurrection and the life. Whoever believes in me, though he die, yet shall he live.*[160] To the women, this must have sounded like a riddle. To Orual, to die before you die meant to stay alive. She knew with everything within her she was not to kill herself. The god's voice, the hearing of it, brought clarity, and Orual hobbles back to the palace in the cover of night.

---

[158] *Ibid.*, 39.

[159] Matthew 16:24, ESV

[160] John 11:25, ESV

THOUGHT QUESTIONS

1. What could Lewis be saying about the humble faith of the common people? What is religion to them?

2. What is the difference between internal and external ugliness? Is there one?

3. Why does Orual think she must commit suicide?

4. What does it mean to you, "to die before you die"?

MOTIF

What's another way to describe Orual's internal veil? How does this relate to us and our spiritual life?

THEME

What is hidden in this chapter?

Chapter 3

THE COMPLAINT

"But," says the Torah, "whenever someone turns to ADONAI, the veil is taken away."[161]

IN THE LAST chapter, Orual removed both her outer veil and her inner one. Through her time in the temple, her vision involving the king, and her suicide attempt, her understanding of herself and the god has increased. Notice that Lewis no longer refers to *the gods* plurally but has instead returned to include *the one* Orual knows. Yes, he is Cupid in the original myth, but more importantly, he is the god of love, and Orual knows his voice. Jesus said that his sheep know his voice and won't follow the voice of a stranger, and what's more, he calls them by name.[162] This personal god knows her.

As Orual reflects on the words of the god, she is reminded of both the Fox's words and those of Socrates. If Socrates said that true wisdom is the skill and practice of death, then Orual realizes that passions and opinions will fall away and die. Now she thinks she understands the words of her father in the dream. "I am Ungit" means she must stop "devouring" and being ugly from the inside.

Orual vows to be upright and virtuous each day. Surely the gods will help! Yet they don't, and Orual falls into old behaviors and patterns without success. Lewis writes, "The natural loves are not self-sufficient" or "kept sweet."[163] Orual cannot be virtuous on her own. Andrew Lazo connects her self-reliance to Modernism, illustrating how the writings of Lewis and J.R.R. Tolkien are full of Modernist qualities like despair and finality, but also

---

[161] II Corinthians 3:16, CJB

[162] John 10:2-5, ESV

[163] *The Four Loves*, 149.

renovation.[164] Perhaps Lewis is highlighting our frail humanness or even the weakness of humanism.

Orual is sure the gods are not helping and will not help her. After all, she has no physical nor inner beauty. It seems that each person is fated from birth to be beautiful in some way, and she is not. Therefore, they will not help her. As Lewis brings in this idea of fatalism, he identifies one more human means of coping in life. We should not turn to ourselves and our strengths to live life as humanism espouses, and neither should we blame fate, as if we have no choice. Orual cannot see that she has always had choice. She assures us that it is her bitter fate or destiny to be ugly in every way. She queries what if "we were made to be dregs and refuse everywhere and everyway?" (283). Her hopelessness seems absolute but for another dream.

As she walks into her room for an afternoon rest, Orual walks into the next dream. She faces a great river, and across from it, the gods' land, a brilliantly colored scene of green meadow, blue sky, and a flock of enormous golden rams. Orual immediately ventures across the river to get some gold wool because then she thinks she would have beauty. But as she emerges from the water, the flock, like "a wall of living gold," stampedes her, yet she is not injured or dead. Unlike the original myth, Orual's task isn't a physical one designed by Venus. It appears to be a spiritual one. Orual explains that the rams did not trample her in rage but in joy, like a force of the Divine Nature.

Within moments in the dream, Orual sees another woman gleaning gold wool from the bushes. How easy for her! Orual reveals much in her next thought: "What I had sought in vain by meeting the joyous and terrible brutes, she took at her leisure. She won without effort what utmost effort would not win for me" (284). "Simple Psyche" had complete faith and trust in the god of the Grey Mountain, and once she was sacrificed by the people of Glome, she was then rescued by Zephyr, carried to the

---

[164] Lazo, "Time to Prepare a Face," 12, 14.

god, and loved by him wholly. Enright says these tasks are harder for Orual as she goes through both exile and trial: "The implication is that Psyche understands how to submit herself to grace but Orual has yet to learn this."[165]

Though Lewis doesn't say, Orual must have woken at this point, for she tells us how she goes about her life and work, even meting out the best and wisest rulings ever when her people come to her for justice. Schakel tells us Orual is unknowingly giving of herself for her country. It is a sacrifice of sorts, though incomplete.[166] She doesn't care about these, however, and comforts herself by reading her own version of how she loved Psyche, the book we are reading. She remains blind to the fact that the loves "cannot remain themselves and do what they promise to do without God's help."[167]

Next, Orual walks into another vision. This one is harsher. She finds herself toiling through a desert, carrying an empty bowl to gather the waters of death as a gift to Ungit. In the scorching heat and blinding sun, Orual feels as if a hundred years has passed. The unending toil reminds us of more than one Greek myth where the gods have punished mortals with futility. In other cultures, a bowl of water is given to one dying so that they may see their reflection and know themselves before death arrives. We already knew that Orual was near the end of her life, but an empty bowl could be symbolic of the emptiness within Orual.

Her desert journey ends as she arrives at a great almost nightmarish mountain. She knows the well of death she seeks is inside. The brilliant light of the sun remains all about her, and she falls to her knees outside. An eagle lands in front of her, asking who she is and what she carries. He does not care that she is Queen of Glome. Orual looks down at the bowl she has carried across the desert and finds that it is now her scroll. Surely, as the

---

[165] Enright, "Transformation," 112.

[166] Schakel, "A Retelling," 12.

[167] *The Four Loves*, 152.

water of death would reflect who she really is, this scroll is all that she is.

The eagle announces that she has come with a complaint against the gods. Orual is surrounded quickly by a crowd of things "like men" that push and pull her inside to a waiting crowd. All the time, shouts of "Bring her in!" echo inside and out. Orual is taken from the hot sunlight to the dark recesses of the mountain.

Generally in literature and scripture, moving from light to dark foreshadows evil to come. Yet, remember Orual's visit to the first mountain. It is where she encountered the strongest love. Psyche chose to abandon her god and husband to save Orual, and she did. And here, Orual undeniably heard and saw the god for the first time. Now, she is *within* the mountain.

She is pushed by the masses to a platform. All becomes dark and silent before a grey light emerges. In the half-light like the twilight of the gods, Orual can see now tens of thousands of faces, including the ghosts of her father, Bardia, and the Fox. The court was full. Veiled in black, the judge commands Orual to be stripped, and she stands old and naked before them all. The judge could be a neutral entity in her dream, or as Schakel believes, it could be herself since she has asked for one repeatedly throughout the story.[168] As she looks at her scroll, it too appears old and shabby. Again, I think this book, that scroll, represents all she is. They are synonymous. She, the judge, commands herself to read the complaint. She must listen.

As Orual unrolls it and looks at her writing, all she sees is a "vile scribble," as if her writing were some immature emotional graffiti, and soon Orual says, "I heard myself reading" (290). Such a simple sentence, but it is critical. Now Orual finally hears herself make the complaint. Manganiello calls it "a monologic babble" that pre-empts any kind of dialogue with the god or judge.[169]

---

[168] Schakel, *Reason and Imagination*, 76-77.
[169] Manganiello, "From Idolatry," 38.

Orual begins with acknowledging that she did meet a real god and did see his house. She argues that if all gods were like that, real and not hidden like Ungit, then she could have borne their presence. But the gods like Ungit and the Shadowbrute are ugly and cannot be seen as they are wrapped in storied legend. She confronts the gods, exclaiming that stories like the Brute devouring the sacrifice are so obscure, how can they be real? How can you have faith in something like that? Of course, she is unable to see that she too was a devourer.

Orual next asks why the gods stole Psyche's love from her. She doesn't say they stole Psyche herself, not yet. Enright distinguishes Orual's jealousy from the two sisters in the original myth, adding that "Orual's jealousy is far more complex; she wishes to be the one to reveal the truth to her sister, having a kind of ownership over her."[170] And this ownership is united with excessive pride stemming from a distorted *storge*.

Yes, we can see Orual's jealousy, but it's more than revealing that the loss of love is so impactful. Consider her life and loss. Orual never had a mother. The only nurturing relationship she had was the grandfatherly one with the Fox. Her father was a true abuser, and no man ever loved her for herself. Only Psyche saw Orual for who she was and chose to love her. So of course, the gods torture Orual with the loss of Psyche's love.

More so, Orual adds that the gods not only use their beauty to entice, but they also take the most beautiful from us. She's convinced that beauty is a key likely because it is something she has never had. "You're a tree in whose shadow we can't thrive" (291).

Man is always lesser in this competition, and more than once, Orual declares that Psyche was "Mine!" She also claims, "I am my own," a statement Lewis often quoted from George MacDonald. MacDonald said, "The one principle of hell is 'I am my own.'"[171]

The judge interrupts her rant, and Orual suddenly knows that she has been reading her complaint over and over and over. A long silence follows. The judge asks her if she received her answer, and Orual says "Yes." She had asked earlier, "How could I want to know it?" or how could she desire to know and acknowledge the gods' existence when Psyche's love was stolen? It needed to be fair, to make sense, and it doesn't. For some reason, Orual still cannot see that Psyche had a choice and that choice was hers only.

THOUGHT QUESTIONS

1. What could being inside the mountain represent for Orual? How does it relate to Arnom's story about Ungit's birth at springtime?

2. When the rams trample her, did Orual die?

3. Why does Orual say the gods are ugly?

4. How do Psyche and Orual each represent both faith and doubt?

THEME

How can we live well if we rely on ourselves only?

---

[171] George MacDonald, *George MacDonald: An Anthology* , ed. C. S. Lewis (New York: MacMillan, 1947), 85.

Chapter 4

PERFECT LOVE

"Now, ADONAI in this text means the Spirit.
And where the Spirit of ADONAI is, there is freedom.
So all of us, with faces unveiled, see as in a mirror the glory of
the Lord; and we are being changed into his very image, from
one degree of glory to the next, by ADONAI the Spirit."[172]

THE DREAM CONTINUES. Orual now knows that "the complaint was the answer" because those were the truest words from within her, the words that had been the center of her life, even controlling her life. With these words, Orual can say that nothing stands between her and the gods any longer. Here, Hood and Myers point out that Orual resembles Job once again. Like Job, she has retracted her accusation.[173] She is now "bareface" and asks, "How can they meet us face to face till we have faces?" (294).

This is such a complicated thought for my students that I always ask them to paraphrase this question, especially in light of what Lewis may mean as a Christian in relation to God. We could say, "How can God meet with me, be with me, until I know who I am, until I know who I am in Him?"

More than one Lewis scholar has pointed out the similarity of Orual's unveiling to Lewis's words in *Letters to Malcolm*. He writes that we have always been known by God, "objects of Divine knowledge," but when we become fully aware of Him, "We have unveiled. Not that any veil could have baffled His sight. The change is in us."[174]

---

[172] II Corinthians 3:17-18, CJB

[173] Hood, "Heroic Orual," 44, and Doris T. Myers, *Bareface,* 14.

[174] Lewis, *Letters to Malcolm*, 32-33.

Immediately, the Fox speaks out and confesses to the judge that he had taught Orual wrongly. The lament that follows is indeed a prolonged confession. He bemoans the fact that he knew the people "got" something from worshipping Ungit. He implies that their simple faith was in fact real in addition to the sacrifices the Priest knew were needed. The gods "will have sacrifice—will have man" (295). I know that sounds barbaric and pagan, but in the Christian sense, the Fox is explaining that God will have us, all of us. He is more disturbed, however, with his deception and confesses that he had fed Orual on words. His Greek wisdom, logic, knowledge—all had failed her and him.

The judge then releases Orual because she had made her accusation and been answered. There was nothing else for her to say or do. She gazes down from the platform, choosing to "end it," flinging herself down to the cave floor. But suicide is not possible here, and somehow the Fox catches her. Orual is astonished at how real and warm he is in this afterlife of a dream. The Fox in turn begs her forgiveness for all the drivel he taught her, yet Orual pleads for his mercy for how she "took" his life. She knows he remained in Glome out of love, and yes, pity for her. He acknowledges that he knew that, but now it's time to go to the true judges. They must answer her complaint.

The Fox leads Orual away from the dark mountain cavern to a special three-walled chamber to wait for her summons by the judges. Filtered sunshine flows into the space from a fourth wall of vines and pillars that lead out into green meadow and shining water. The desert is no more, but could this be the water of death Orual was to gather?

The Fox then serves as guide to the living murals, movies even, that cover the three walls. At first, Orual is hesitant. She feels the pictures might serve as a mirror to her ugliness (297). Arnell points out that "the beauty of the pictures educates her in a way that Psyche's beauty could not."[175] Perhaps it is the perspective they provide as distant replicas.

The first captures the image of a woman walking to the river's edge and then binding her feet with her belt. Surely this is Orual. But no, Orual looks and recognizes Psyche in all her beauty. Remember that Orual feels that beauty is the one thing the gods chose to keep from her. We also remember that the god of the Grey Mountain told Orual she too would be Psyche.

They move to the next picture as it comes to life. This portrays a dim image of Psyche in rags and chains, sorting seeds with the utmost concentration as a swarm of ants aid her in her task. Orual marvels, and they watch a third image of Psyche gathering the gold wool from the gods' rams. It is the same as Orual's waking vision in the previous chapter but without Orual.

The next scene is also familiar. Orual sees herself as a shadow next to Psyche as they toil through the desert. Psyche carries her empty bowl while Orual hugs her scroll. Somehow Psyche is tired yet happy, singing as she makes her way, "merry and good in heart" (300). As Psyche arrives at the mountain, the eagle takes her bowl and returns it full of the water of death. This alone might imply that Psyche is already dead, if she had indeed been given the water and tasted it. At the same time, Orual's shadow disappeared.

Again, Orual is staggered by Psyche's contentment and joy through every trial. How could she be happy? The Fox explains that someone else bore her anguish, and it was Orual. Orual is stunned. He reminds her that the gods and men are all part of each other, thus Orual carried the burden and hardship of Psyche's "impossible" tasks. So reminiscent of I John 3:16, it almost seems as if Orual not only carried her sister's burden but also carried the burden of ugliness.

The Fox queries whether she "would have rather had justice." And of course Orual says no. As a queen, a ruler of men, she knows how men behave including herself. She makes reference

---

[175] Arnell, "On Beauty," 30.

again to the selfish nature of Batta and Redival and herself. She doesn't need justice anymore.

They turn to the third wall where Psyche is descending to Hades for the final impossible task of retrieving a box of beauty from Persephone as a gift to Ungit or Venus. Unlike the original myth, there is no deceit involved in Psyche's ordeal. Ungit has not placed a deadly sleep within this casket. Psyche must never speak to a soul as part of the test, and the Fox's narration is strangely reminiscent of the first Priest's style, resembling more myth than fact. Yet in these words, logic is laid aside as the Fox relays how Ungit is within each of us and we must bear her son and die in childbirth or change ourselves.

In other words, we must surrender all that we are, and in Orual's case, all of our ugliness, in order to become beautiful. It might sound mythic, yet it is a beautiful metamorphosis. It is a return to the Greek meaning of Psyche's name—soul or butterfly. *And whoever does not take his cross and follow me is not worthy of me. Whoever finds his life will lose it, and whoever loses his life for my sake will find it.*[176]

As Psyche journeys, she walks through myriad temptations. Enright likens her to Peter who was asked to acknowledge Christ three times.[177] Crowds like those outside the palace walls once called to her for healing cheer her once again, demanding to worship her. Surprisingly, the Fox appears next in the scene, tempting Psyche to disbelieve and remember Greek wisdom. Next comes a shadowy woman who pleads passionately to Psyche to turn aside and come with her. The mysterious figure drips blood from her arm, and Orual knows it is herself.

Without her veil, both the real and the symbolic, Orual can now see what she did to Psyche and how she caused her sister anguish. The Fox too acknowledges that together they were Psyche's enemies. Enright feels Lewis suggests Psyche must

---

[176] Matthew 10:38-39, ESV

[177] Enright, "Transformation," 113.

"keep her eyes focused on what she must do and not be distracted or dissuaded from it even though pity or misguided human love urges her to turn aside."[178]

In the most poetic language, the Fox, that is Lewis, next details how mankind will someday be able to truly see how beautiful the gods are. And, more and more people will come to see! "Nothing is yet in its true form" not even the past, because we are still in the process of seeing. But suddenly from outside the chamber, the Fox and Orual hear shouts that Psyche is coming with the gift of beauty. It is no longer a living image on a wall, but Psyche herself, for she has succeeded in not only her tasks, but also in love, the charity Lewis speaks of.

The Fox leads Orual out of the chamber, what had moments before been a judgment seat, a dark cavern, then an honest account of her life. They stand outside in the grassy courtyard before a pool of water with a mountain sky above. Yes, a mountain. Yes, that God of the mountain. And Psyche comes, and Orual falls at her feet, wholeheartedly repenting for her selfishness— "Never again will I call you mine; but all there is of me shall be yours" (305). Psyche draws her up and reminds her that she has not given the gift of beauty to Ungit yet. Schakel explains that here Orual has removed "the veil of pretense and defense," anything that has come between herself and the divine.[179]

Yes, we remember. Orual is Ungit, has become her. As Psyche holds her hands, she burns Orual with the same touch of the immortal, the divine. She is radiant and "a thousand times more her very self" (306). Yes, the gift of beauty has been given. Orual is replete with joy, then she becomes aware of something greater. Was it a brighter light, a deeper color about her, a quaking within herself? Voices again announce. This time the god is coming. So much, so much Orual has come to understand. She is

---

[178] *Ibid.*, 112.

[179] Schakel, "A Retelling," 12.

overwhelmed and already feels that she has been given all that she could ever desire as she and Psyche are reconciled forever.

Psyche brings Orual to the edge of the pool as the air itself grows brighter in the sunshine. The god's presence increases moment by moment, and Orual says that she feels as if she's being "unmade." This scene mirrors other moments of conversion in Lewis's fiction like that of Jane Studdock in *That Hideous Strength*.[180] He is coming, and everything exists for his sake. Orual knows this. No more questions, no more doubt, no more resistance. His presence is piercing her as she looks down. She sees herself in the pool, naked and unmade, next to clothed Psyche, yet they appear the same. The god speaks and says to her, not "You shall be," but "You also are Psyche" (308).

She looks up to see him and wakes fully from the vision back in the palace gardens. The transformation is complete. The God of Love came just for her to complete what He promised. Orual is no longer ugly in any way but is wholly beautiful. His presence, His love is perfect and simple and transforming. Could this have been a baptism in the water's reflection? Possibly, but it seems more profound and final. The only water of death present has gone as the old washed away.

Every barrier is gone. Orual is at peace. Before her death a few days later, she confesses, "Before your face questions die away" (308), and Orual's life is brought to completion.

Lazo aptly reminds us that Orual's death is a beginning, an idea that echoes through Lewis's writing.[181] In his fiction, Lewis's characters come to realize that their lives are not at an end. Tor the King in *Perelandra* says, "It is but the wiping out of a false start in order that the world may *then* begin."[182] In *The Last Battle*, the Narnian Earth devolves as Aslan's Country emerges:

---

[180] Schakel, *Reason and Imagination*, 85-86.

[181] Lazo, "Time to Prepare a Face," 19-22.

[182] as quoted in Lazo and *Perelandra* (New York: Scribner, 2003), 182.

"...it was only the beginning of the real story. All
their life in this world and all their adventures in
Narnia had only been the cover and the title page:
now at last they were beginning Chapter One of the
Great Story which no one on earth had read: which
goes on forever: in which every chapter is better
than the one before."[183]

So too Lewis's autobiography and *The Four Loves* echo with
the "pointer" that we have been made for more than we can
imagine.

"Perhaps, for many of us, all experience merely
defines, so to speak, the shape of that gap where our
love of God ought to be...to become increasingly
aware of our unawareness till we feel like men who
should stand beside a great cataract and hear no
noise, or like a man in a story who looks in a mirror
and finds no face there, or a man in a dream who
stretches out his hand to visible objects and gets so
sensation of touch. To know that one is dreaming is
to be no longer perfectly asleep. But for news of the
fully waking world you must go to my betters."[184]

THOUGHT QUESTIONS

1. How has Orual given of herself for Psyche?
2. Like Job, Orual's story began with a lament. How has
Lewis returned to this parallel? (see Job 42)

---

[183] *The Last Battle*, 210-211.

[184] as quoted in Lazo and *The Four Loves*, 180.

MOTIF

How has Lewis deepened his story with dreams, especially in Part 2 and the final chapter?

THEME

What do you think of Lewis's statement in his Introduction to *The Four Loves:*"the states in which a man is 'nearest' to God are those in which he is most surely and swiftly approaching his final union with God, vision of God, and enjoyment of God"?

Conclusion

There is no fear in love.
On the contrary, love that has achieved its goal gets rid of fear,
because fear has to do with punishment; the person who keeps
fearing has not been brought to maturity in regard to love. We
ourselves love now because he loved us first.[185]

COMING TO CHRIST is no panacea, but if C.S. Lewis were to tell us a tale of how pain and doubt were inevitable and unavoidable in a life of belief in God, who would willingly listen? It's one thing to share personal experience or to preach a lesson, but in fiction, an author and his audience might just be left with a moralizing and probably unlikeable character instead.

Most fiction features at least one appealing character—the one you cheer for, stumble with, return to. Therein lies one of the trickiest elements in *Till We Have Faces*. Perhaps one of the most exasperating characters of all of Lewis's novels, Orual is an unlikely blend for a central character. At the beginning of the tale, she is practically an orphaned girl without love or looks, and so we naturally pity her. By the time Psyche is born, it seems that Orual now has a purpose in life. In spite of her abusive father, she can now care for Psyche and be loved in return by Psyche and the Fox.

Yet the same thing that brings joy to Orual also brings the most pain, and we begin to dislike Orual as she denies the truth of Psyche's sincere faith and even the god who revealed himself to her. Orual's long-term obstinacy and manipulation is offensive to us. We are frustrated by her resistance. But does this make her a lesser character?

---

[185] I John 4:18-19, CJB

Gwyneth Hood asks us to view her as an admirable heroine. She "strives to change for the better the ugly and undesirable situation around her."[186] And there are moments of hope. When she ascends the mountain with Bardia, her heart delights in the beauty that surrounds her. In spite of the errand of grief, her heart is responsive. This is not just a sensitivity to nature, but a means by which God can speak to her.

As her audience, we too hope that she might know God. Hope might also spur her to pray and ask the gods for their help after her first visit to the Grey Mountain. Yet Orual hears and feels nothing after hours of prayer. When we look at her in those moments, we can see that she is likely manipulating her religion. Orual wants things her own way because she only understands how to do things, to make things happen, in order to get something else. Her prayers are based on herself, not in a sincere relationship with God.

She selfishly demands an answer, and it must come in the way she chooses. Orual's wrestling is paralleled in James 1:6-8 (ESV): *But let him ask in faith, with no doubting, for the one who doubts is like a wave of the sea that is driven and tossed by the wind. For that person must not suppose that he will receive anything from the Lord; he is a double-minded man, unstable in all his ways.* Doubt is a harsh teacher, and it's probably because it stems from our own selfishness. With doubt in the way, Orual cannot see or hear the gods. And yet she continues to try.

As most of us do then, if we cannot hear God, we blame Him. Orual declares, "The gods never send us this invitation to delight so readily or so strongly as when they are preparing some new agony. We are their bubbles; they blow us big before they prick us" (97). This same fatalism is echoed in James 1:13-15 (ESV): *Let no one say when he is tempted, 'I am being tempted by God,' for God cannot be tempted with evil, and he himself tempts no one. But each person is tempted when he is lured and enticed by his*

---

[186] Hood, "Heroic Orual," 44.

own desire. Then desire when it has conceived gives birth to sin, and sin when it is fully grown brings forth death.

As James writes, Orual is motivated by her own desire. Not one of us is helped by blaming God. Yet we cannot be perfectly wrong, and neither can Orual. Orual's domineering selfishness is key, and Ansit seems to be the only one to recognize it fully: "You're full fed. Gorged with other men's lives, women's too: Bardia's, mine the Fox's, your sister's—both your sisters'" (266). Orual is angered and repulsed by this, but she can see it is true. Whether her obsessive love for Psyche or her controlling love for Bardia, Orual's idea of love is wholly tainted. It brings death to all.

And so, how can we like a character who has damaged so many, including herself? This is a distinctive point of Lewis's tale. We don't have to like Orual or agree with her or even hope for her, but we do need to see ourselves in her. Lewis wrote to his friend Clyde Kilby that Orual was "an instance, a 'case,' of human affection in its natural condition: true, tender, suffering, but in the long run, tyrannically possessive and ready to turn to hatred when the beloved ceases to be its possession."[187] If Orual is an instance in Lewis's words, then we are liable. If we read this myth as story only, then we have lost its moral lesson and the pending redemption. "It is largely through the redemption of Orual that Lewis explores the depth and complexity of the three natural human loves (*storge, philia,* and *eros*) and the salvation possible even for those who, like Orual, 'know not what they do.'"[188]

At the end of her reign, Orual finally realizes the futility of hiding from herself, "I did and I did and I did, and what does it matter that I did?" (236). She has no concept of what trust nor rest is. She has struggled with this from the beginning. Just as Psyche exemplifies a working faith, Orual finds it hard to trust. On her first visit to the mountain, Orual declares she almost came to a full belief (120). The almost is conscious doubt. She knows Psyche is

---

[187] see footnote 61

[188] Enright, "Transformation," 97.

certain, and she knows she, Orual, is not. It is a sickening feeling, and Orual is filled with both horror and grief at the gulf between them, immediately blaming the gods, instead of herself. Lewis wrote to Katherine Farrer that this is "the story of every nice, affectionate agnostic whose dearest one suddenly 'gets religion', or even every luke-warm Christian whose dearest gets a Vocation."[189] The divide is clear.

Moreover, when Orual returns to the mountain the second time determined to forcibly remove Psyche, she cannot see Psyche's perspective nor can she truly see Psyche's joy. Though Orual is certain she is right, she is blind. I John 2:8-11 says this is *because the darkness is passing away and the true light is already shining. Whoever says he is in the light and hates his brother is still in darkness. Whoever loves his brother abides in the light, and in him there is no cause for stumbling. But whoever hates his brother is in the darkness and walks in the darkness, and does not know where he is going, because the darkness has blinded his eyes.* Here, John reveals what Orual cannot know of herself yet—that she "hates" Psyche. This hatred incites her blindness, and by novel's end, Orual herself confesses to Psyche that she has always been a "craver," loving her only "selflessly" (305).

As Part II begins, Orual tells us that the gods began their surgery and reopened her wounds. Her blindness cannot remain. "Before the end, she perceives that no lasting happiness will reach her until her own ugly and undesirable nature is transformed."[190] This surgery is an image of pain, but it's also an image of rescue. The gods (God) will not allow her to hide behind the guise of "Queen." All of Orual must be seen.

Ansit is the first to recognize that Orual both loves and devours just as Ungit does in the Great Sacrifice (265). Within Orual's dream and journey deep into the earth without her veil,

---

[189] C.S. Lewis to Katherine Farrer, April 2, 1955, in Hooper, *C.S. Lewis: A Complete Guide*, 249.

[190] *Ibid.*

Orual comes to understand who she is, the very thing she has never understood—Ungit.

Before the dream, Arnom has just told Orual that Ungit was "the earth, the womb and mother of all living things" (270). And here Orual is, deep within the earth, seeing the reflection of Ungit in the mirror. Ungit is symbolic of our own ugliness, our selfishness, our sinfulness, not just Orual's. Though she wakes immediately, Orual's first reaction is to try to kill herself because she knows she cannot "fix" her ugliness. Little does she know that her rescue has begun.

In the midst of her final dream, Orual is answered by the gods, for now she knows without riddle they have always been there. Once Psyche gives her the gift of beauty and the God of the mountain appears and speaks to her, her ugliness is washed away. Orual had not been able to see until the end that love, the real love of Charity, reveals truth incessantly, so that we can be like God. Yes, it takes all of Orual's life to come to this point, and even then, it is in a dream, yet now she can love herself and be loved by God fully. I John 3:2 says, *Beloved, we are God's children now, and what we will be has not yet appeared; but we know that when he appears we shall be like him, because we shall see him as he is.*

Bibliography

Arnell, Carla A. "On Beauty, Justice, and the Sublime in C. S. Lewis's *Till We Have Faces," Christianity and Literature* 52, no.1 (Autumn 2002): 23-32.

Barfield, Owen. *Saving the Appearances: A Study in Idolatry.* London: Faber and Faber, 1957.

Bulfinch, Thomas. "Cupid and Psyche." *The Age of Fable.* New York: Review of Reviews, 1913; Bartleby.com, 2000. www.bartleby.com/bulfinch/

Chesterton, G.K. "The Ethics of Elfland." In *Orthodoxy.* London: John Lane Company, 1908. 81-118.

Como, James. *C. S. Lewis: A Very Short Introduction.* Oxford: Oxford University Press, 2019.

Davidman, Joy. *Out of My Bone: The Letters of Joy Davidman.* Edited by Don W. King. Grand Rapids: Eerdmans, 2009.

Dunne, John Anthony. "'Nothing Beautiful Hides Its Face': The Hiddenness of Esther in C. S. Lewis' *Till We Have Faces.'" Sehnsucht: The C. S. Lewis Journal* 9 (2015): 75-88.

Enright, Nancy. "C. S. Lewis's *Till We Have Faces* and the Transformation of Love." *Logos: A Journal of Catholic Thought & Culture* 14, no. 4 (Fall 2011): 92-115.

Glover, Donald E. "The Magician's Book: That's Not Your Story." *Studies in the Literary Imagination* 22, no. 2 (Fall 1989): 217-225.

Glyer, Diana Pavlac. "Joy Davidman Lewis: Author, Editor and Collaborator," *Mythlore: A Journal of J.R.R. Tolkien, C. S. Lewis, Charles Williams, and Mythopoeic Literature* 22, no.2 (1998): 10-17.

Helfers, James P. "A Time for Joy: The Ancestry and Apologetic Force of C. S. Lewis' Sehnsucht." *Sehnsucht: The C. S. Lewis Journal* 1 (2007): 7-18.

Hood, Gwenyth. "Heroic Orual and the Tasks of Psyche," *Mythlore: A Journal of J.R.R. Tolkien, C. S. Lewis, Charles Williams, and Mythopoeic Literature* 27, no.3 (2009): 43-70.

Hooper, Walter. *C. S. Lewis: A Complete Guide to His Life & Works*. San Francisco: HarperCollins, 1996.

Huttar, Charles. "What C. S. Lewis Really Did to 'Cupid and Psyche.'" *Sehnsucht: The C. S. Lewis Journal* 3 (2009): 33-50.

Kilby, Clyde S. *The Christian World of C. S. Lewis*. Grand Rapids: Eerdmans, 1964.

Lazo, Andrew. "'Time to Prepare a Face': Mythology Comes of Age," *Mythlore: A Journal of J.R.R. Tolkien, C. S. Lewis, Charles Williams, and Mythopoeic Literature* 35, no. 2 (2017): 5-24.

Lewis, C. S. *The Discarded Image: An Introduction to Medieval and Renaissance Literature*. Cambridge: Cambridge University Press, 1964.

———. *An Experiment in Criticism*. Cambridge: Cambridge University Press, 1961.

———. *The Four Loves*. New York: Harcourt, 1960.

———. *The Last Battle: A Story for Children*. New York: Scholastic, 1995.

———. *Letters to Malcolm: Chiefly on Prayer*. New York: Harcourt, 1964.

———. *Mere Christianity*. New York: Macmillan, 1960.

———. *The Pilgrim's Regress*. Grand Rapids: Baker, 1958.

———. *Prince Caspian*. New York: Scholastic, 1995.

———. *The Silver Chair*. New York, Scholastic, 1995.

———. *On Stories and Other Essays on Literature*, Edited by Walter Hooper. Orlando: Harcourt, 1982.

———. *Studies in Medieval and Renaissance Literature*. Cambridge: Cambridge University Press, 1980.

———. *Surprised by Joy: The Shape of My Early Life*. New York: Harcourt, 1956.

———. *Till We Have Faces*. New York: Harcourt Brace, 1980.

MacDonald, George. *George MacDonald: An Anthology*. Edited by C. S. Lewis. New York: MacMillan, 1947.

Manganiello, Dominic. "*Till We Have Faces*: From Idolatry to Revelation." *Mythlore: A Journal of J.R.R. Tolkien, C. S. Lewis, Charles Williams, and Mythopoeic Literature* 23, no.1 (2000): 31-44.

Markos, Louis. *Restoring Beauty: The Good, the True, and the Beautiful in the Writings of C. S. Lewis.* Downers Grove, Illinois: Biblica, 2010.

Myers, Doris T. *Bareface: A Guide to C. S. Lewis's Last Novel.* Columbia: University of Missouri Press, 2004.

Root, Jerry, and Mark Neal. *The Surprising Imagination of C. S. Lewis: An Introduction.* Nashville: Abingdon Press, 2015.

Schakel, Peter J. *Reason and Imagination in C. S. Lewis: A Study of Till We Have Faces.* Grand Rapids: Eerdmans, 1984.

Schakel, Peter J. "A Retelling within a Myth Retold: The Priest of Essur and Lewisian Mythopoetics." *Mythlore* 9, no.4 (1983): 10-12.

Spingarn, J. E. "The New Criticism" in *Criticism in America, Its Function and Status: Essays.* Edited by W.C. Brownell, et al. New York: Harcourt, 1924.

Watson, Thomas Ramey. "Enlarging Augustinian Systems: C. S. Lewis's *The Great Divorce* and *Till We Have Faces.*" *Renascence* 46, no.3 (1994): 175.

Wood, Ralph C. "Doubt about the Goodness of God in C. S. Lewis's *Till We Have Faces.*" *Literature and Theology.* Nashville: Abingdon Press, 2008. 69-86.

About the Author

Christine Norvell is an author, speaker, and longtime educator. She graduated from Faulkner University with a Masters in Humanities and teaches high school literature in an online classical Christian community. A mother of three boys, she reads, writes, and teaches from her home in Oklahoma with the family cat Pippin.

If you'd like to read more about her nonfiction and fiction endeavors, sign up for Christine's monthly newsletter at www.thylyre.com, or follow her on www.facebook.com/thylyre and Twitter @thy_lyre.

If you, your book club, church, or class benefitted from using this companion, kindly leave a review on Amazon, Goodreads, or any book retailer site.

Made in the USA
Coppell, TX
08 June 2022

78613992R00111